CONTENTS

© Scripture Union 2017
First published 2017

ISBN 978 1 78506 559 0

Scripture Union, Trinity House, Opal Court, Opal Drive
Fox Milne, Milton Keynes, MK15 0DF, UK
Email: info@scriptureunion.org.uk
Website: www.scriptureunion.org.uk

Performing Licence
If you wish to perform any of the sketches in this book, you
are free to do so without charge, providing the performance is
undertaken in an amateur context. The purchase of this book
constitutes a licence granting the right to perform the pieces
for no financial gain. Those wishing to engage in commercial or
professional performances should make a separate approach
in writing to Scripture Union.

British Library Cataloguing-in-Publication Data. A catalogue
record of this book is available from the British Library.

Printed and bound in India by Replika Press Pvt Ltd

Writers: Sue Clutterham, Becca Dean, Karen Herrick,
Alex Taylor, Gemma Willis
Artwork: Tim Charnick
Design: Martin Lore

Scripture Union is an international Christian charity
working with churches in more than 130 countries.

Thank you for purchasing this book. Any profits from this book
support SU in England and Wales to bring the good news of
Jesus Christ to children, young people and families and to
enable them to meet God through the Bible and prayer.

Find out more about our work and how you can get involved at:
www.scriptureunion.org.uk (England and Wales)
www.suscotland.org.uk (Scotland)
www.suni.co.uk (Northern Ireland)
www.scriptureunion.org (USA)
www.su.org.au (Australia)

Hello!

Christmas is a wonderful time of year for people of all ages to celebrate the coming of God's Son.

But, when you explore the same story every year, it's easy to run out of ideas.

This fabulous, new resource book is full of Christmas-themed prayer ideas, games, crafts, all-age talks, monologues and so much more.

All of the activities contained within this book are brand new, easy to use, tried and tested and can be easily adapted to suit groups of all ages and contexts.

So, now it's over to you – may God bless you in your ministry!

The Scripture Union Resources Team

Ten exciting and easily-explained crafts for all ages. Some messy, some sticky, some done quickly, some done slowly – all with a connection to the Christmas story, from Advent to the wise men. Within each activity, you will also find suggestions for how it could be used within the context of an all-age service.

CRAFTS

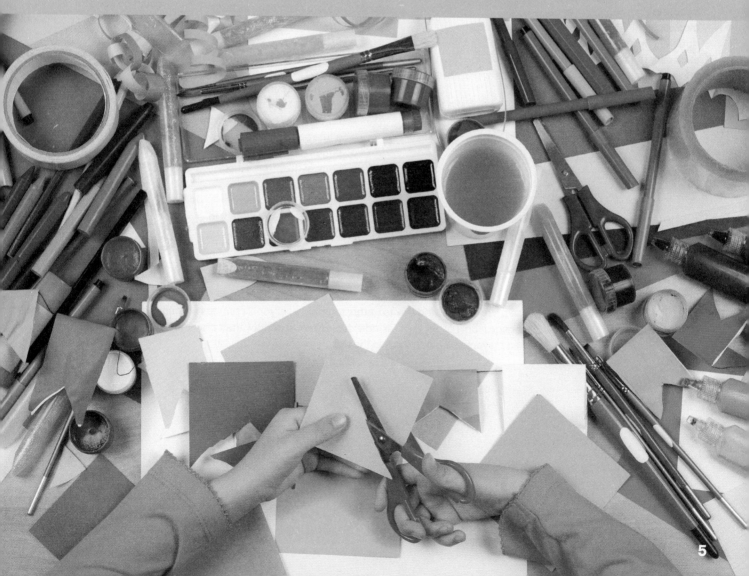

ADVENT PRAYER BOX

Description: an Advent zig-zag book in a box to encourage prayer and reflection
Difficulty level: ✽ ✽
Bible link: 1 Thessalonians 5:16–18

YOU WILL NEED:

- craft box with lid approximately 9cm square
- craft paper or stickers to decorate
- glue stick
- double-sided tape
- stick on letters 'a-d-v-e-n-t'
- stick on numbers 1 to 25
- A2 cartridge paper
- pens and pencils
- scissors

INSTRUCTIONS

- Decorate the box lid with craft papers, stickers and 'a-d-v-e-n-t' letters.
- Cut two long strips, 7.5cm wide (or a little smaller than the inner size of your box) from the A2 cartridge paper. Fold each into eight equal sections.
- Use double-sided tape to fasten together one end square from each strip, to create one long strip of paper.
- Using the folds, make a zig-zag book.
- Count 13 sections (each with two sides) and cut off the remainder. This will give you a title page plus 25 individual pages (using the front and back of the strip). Check before cutting!
- Number the pages, fold up the book and store it in the box.
- Each day of Advent, use a page of the book to encourage prayer and thanks. On alternate days, drawings could be made of the Christmas story (eg a dove, Mary, Joseph, a star, Jesus in the manger, shepherds, magi, gifts of the magi, a stable, Bethlehem, a candle (light of the world), a crown). The days in between could be used for drawings of thanks or praise for people and things.

Variations:
Use at different times of year for other themes. Try a round box with round gift tags tied together.

Easier options:
Decorate the box with stickers. Use individual pages to create a box of prayers.

ALL-AGE EXTRAS:
Use a large decorated box to gather together everyone's prayers of thanks and praise. Give out large luggage labels or gift tags for individuals to write or draw their prayers. Have people bring forward their prayers and place them in the box.

ADVENT PRAYER TREE

Description: Advent activity to encourage prayers of gratitude. This activity can be used at home as something to be revisited each day during Advent, or in a group context, where day 1 is discussed and completed together and the others sent home to be completed over the next few weeks.

Difficulty level: ✳

Bible link: 1 Thessalonians 5:16–18

YOU WILL NEED:

- 24 green glass pebbles or card circles
- small box or bag
- A4 black or dark card
- small star
- permanent marker pen
- strong PVA glue or glue dots
- sweets, eg dolly mixtures (optional)

INSTRUCTIONS

- Use the permanent marker to write the numbers 1 to 24 on the glass pebbles.
- Talk about the meaning of Advent – that we prepare for Christmas, but also for Jesus coming again one day. Explain that each time you add a glass pebble to the tree you will say a thank-you prayer for a person or situation that comes to mind that day.
- Place all but the number 1 pebble into the box or bag for safe keeping.
- Using the glue dots or PVA glue to attach the pebbles to the card, beginning with the first pebble at the top, create a triangular tree, adding a glass prayer pebble each day to the picture.
- Each row will have one more pebble than the last. After six rows, use the remaining three pebbles to create a trunk.

- Add a star at the top of the tree for day 25.
- Add dolly mixture presents as a surprise for the final day.

Variations:
- You could also use the pebbles to pray asking for God's blessing or help.
- Create a smaller non-Advent tree of three rows for immediate prayers in a group. Each child could take turns to pray as they add a glass pebble.
- Or you could use one tree for a group to help them pray, but not number the pebbles.

Easier options:
Don't glue down the pebbles but just lay them on the card.

ALL-AGE EXTRAS:

Create a larger tree with circles of card. Give out circles of card and pens to each person as they arrive. For prayers in the service, ask each to write or draw a prayer on the card and bring it to the front to create a congregational prayer tree.

MARBLED NATIVITY SCENE

Description: using marbling ink and silhouettes to create a nativity scene
Difficulty level: ✻✻
Bible link: Luke 2:1–7

YOU WILL NEED:
- shallow tray, eg aluminium food container with water
- A5 white card or thick cartridge paper
- marbling ink
- cocktail stick or skewer
- thin black card
- templates from page 87
- scissors
- glue stick

INSTRUCTIONS
- Drop two or three coloured marbling inks onto the surface of the water.
- Swirl the inks carefully with a cocktail stick or skewer.
- Carefully lay the card on the surface of the water, ensuring there are no air bubbles.
- Allow the ink to absorb into the card for a few seconds, then carefully lift from the water to dry.
- Use the templates from page 87 to cut a Bethlehem scene or manger from black card.
- Glue the silhouette onto the marbled paper.

Variations:
Try out different nativity scenes with your own silhouettes.

Easier options:
Use pre-bought marbled or decorated paper.

ALL-AGE EXTRAS:
Demonstrate marbling. Ink, water and paper are very simple things, but in the hands of an artist they become something special. With marbling anyone can produce a beautiful image. This is much like the Christian life – how can our lives be something special, something beautiful? From the moment Jesus was born, he led a perfect Spirit-filled, godly life that made a way for us to be close to God and to be filled with the Spirit. We are made beautiful as our sins are washed away, in Jesus. In marbling, it is the importance of the oil that keeps the colour on the surface of the paper. In our lives, we need God's Spirit to help us so that our lives will be beautiful.

ENGRAVED CHRISTMAS STORY

Description: retelling the Christmas story through four symbols drawn onto aluminium

Difficulty level: ✱ ✱ ✱

Bible link: Matthew 1:18 – 2:12; Luke 2:8–20

YOU WILL NEED:

- rectangular aluminium storage container (without pattern on the base)
- craft scissors
- biro
- permanent markers in a range of colours
- old newspaper or magazine
- black electrician's tape

INSTRUCTIONS

- Cut the sides away from the aluminium container (adult only to do this, be careful of sharp edges) and recycle safely.
- Keep the base. If needed, bind the sharp edges with electrician's tape.
- Place the sheet of aluminium onto a newspaper or magazine (if you don't it will be difficult to get a good image with the biro).
- Use the biro to press on and draw two lines that split the aluminium sheet into four equal spaces.
- In the first space, draw a simple angel. Tell of the angel's visit to Mary.
- In the second space, draw a simple heart. Tell of God's love for the world that he gave his only Son to be born and die for us.
- In the third space, draw a simple star. Tell of the visit of the magi, who followed a star to see Jesus.
- In the last space, draw a simple crown. Tell of the shepherds who visited the baby Jesus, born as King and Saviour of the world.
- Turn the aluminium sheet over, so that there are ridges where you have drawn to act as barriers for colouring.
- Using the permanent pens, colour in the symbols.

Variations:

- Make two engraved stories and fasten them back to back with double-sided tape, to create a Christmas tree decoration.
- Use a circular container for just one symbol.

Easier options:

Use recycled plastic (cut from large plastic milk containers) instead of aluminium with permanent marker pens, or use white card and felt tips for a simpler craft.

ALL-AGE EXTRAS:

Just as the markers leave a permanent image on the metal, so too the Christmas story leaves a message that stays with us. How can we 'colour in' the story to make it more visible for others to see it? How can we live the story of the angels; live with God's love in our hearts; shine so that our lives clearly reflect Jesus and act as God's children – as heirs of the kingdom?

CRAFTS **05**

WIRED RIBBON ANGELS

Description: hanging decoration

Difficulty level: ✹ ✹ ✹

Bible link: Luke 1:26–38; Matthew 1:20,21; 2:13,19; Luke 2:8–15

YOU WILL NEED:

- 6cm-wide wired florists ribbon, approximately 12cm in length
- coloured net 12cm x 10cm
- strong thread (eg pearl) and needle
- metal keyring circle
- craft scissors
- metallic thread (optional)

INSTRUCTIONS

- Thread the needle and knot the end of the thread securely.
- Starting at one end of the wired ribbon, stitch running stitch along the top of the ribbon to end.
- Pull thread tight to gather ribbon to form the angel body, and secure the end of the thread.
- Stitch the keyring head onto the back of the wired ribbon until it stays upright (about 10 stitches).

- Take the coloured net and gather it in the centre to create wings.
- Stitch through the gathers then stitch the wings onto the back of the ribbon (until secure).
- Tie metallic thread onto the angel to hang it up.

Variations:
Try out different-sized angels with fabric instead of ribbon.

Easier options:
Try using crêpe paper instead of ribbon.

ALL-AGE EXTRAS:

Angels are God's messengers. Angels brought Mary unexpected news that she would bear God's child. Angels appeared to Joseph to tell him not to be afraid to marry Mary, to warn him to move away from Bethlehem to Egypt to escape Herod and then again to return to Israel. Angels also appeared to the shepherds to herald the good news of Jesus' birth. Use an acrostic to teach:

Angels **a**nnounce and affirm

Remind us **n**ot to be afraid

They bring **g**ood news

They **e**ncourage

They **l**aud and honour (praise)

Angels **s**erve God

How can we be God's messengers today?

CRAFTS **06**

NAMES OF JESUS DECORATION

Description:
decorative hangar
Difficulty level: ✽ ✽
Bible link: Isaiah 9:6

YOU WILL NEED:

- four different-coloured A6 pieces of card
- four pre-cut strips saying: 'Wonderful Counsellor', 'Mighty God', 'Everlasting Father', 'Prince of Peace'
- images of an ear, mountains, sun, moon and stars and a dove, from page 88
- colouring pens and pencils
- paper washi tape
- sticky stars
- glue stick
- 11 coloured paper clips
- hole punch

INSTRUCTIONS

- Use paper washi tape to edge each of the four pieces of card.
- Colour the pictures and stick one onto each card.
- Match the phrases with the pictures, and stick down.
- Use a hole punch to make holes at the top and bottom of the first three cards, and at the top of the last card.
- Decorate with sticky stars.
- Fasten each card together in order with paper clips.
- Join five paper clips together to create a hanging cord and fasten at the top.

Variations:
Use craft foam for a sturdier decoration.

Easier options:
Omit using washi tape. Fasten together with paper fasteners or thread.

ALL-AGE EXTRAS:

Jesus has many names in the Bible, but this verse helps us to understand something of what was foretold many years before his birth and how Jesus helps us. (Use the images of an ear, mountains, sun, moon and stars and dove to illustrate.)
Wonderful Counsellor – Jesus listens to us and helps us sort out problems.
Mighty God – Jesus is strong when we are weak.
Everlasting Father – Jesus is always there for us; He is our heavenly Father who cares for us beyond any human love.
Prince of Peace – Jesus comes to bring peace in our lives and in our world.

CRAFTS 07

JARS OF JOY

Description: lights in decorated glass jars
Difficulty level: ✽
Bible link: Luke 1: 39–56; Luke 2:9–20; Matthew 2:1–10

YOU WILL NEED:
- 1 clean, empty glass jar
- battery-powered small lights
- *either* fabric, buttons, glue
- *or* glass pens and self-adhesive jewels
- *or* glass paint, paper plate, small sponge, self-adhesive jewels
- twine to hang jar

INSTRUCTIONS
- Decide which medium you are going to use to decorate your glass jar.
- Gather together all your materials.
- *To use fabric and buttons,* wrap a strip of fabric around the jar, overlapping slightly and secure with craft glue or glue dots. Then add buttons, sequins etc to decorate further.
- *To use glass pens,* carefully draw your designs onto the glass and leave your design to dry. Follow instructions on pen for setting the paint. When the paint is set, add the self-adhesive jewels.
- *To use glass paints,* place a small amount of two or three colours onto a paper plate. Using a small piece of sponge, dab the colours onto the outside of the glass, overlapping them so that the colours blend together. Leave to dry, then follow instructions on paint for setting colours. When the paint is set, add the self-adhesive jewels.
- Once dry, securely tie the twine around the neck of the jar and make a secure loop across the top, so that the jar will hang up.
- Gently push the short length of lights into the jar.
- Turn on the switch and you have made a jar full of joy!

Variations:
- Try different techniques to decorate your joy jars.
- Display three different-sized jars together for real effect.

Easier options:
Use battery-powered 'candles' as an alternative.

ALL-AGE EXTRAS:
Use five joy jars to talk about the joy of the birth of Jesus. Elizabeth was joyful when Mary visited her and told her the news of Jesus' birth; Mary sang a joyful song to God in praise; the angels joyfully proclaimed the good news of Jesus' birth; the shepherds were full of joy when they saw Jesus; the magi were full of joy when they found Jesus. The Christmas story is full of joyful news. What joyful news do you have in your life? How can we be more joyful?

CRAFTS **08**

BEADED STAR

Description: beaded star decoration
Difficulty level: ✱
Bible link: Matthew 2:1–10

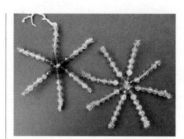

YOU WILL NEED:
- two metallic pipe cleaners
- craft scissors
- 36 coloured 6mm faceted beads
- hanging thread (optional)

INSTRUCTIONS
- Cut each pipe cleaner in half (be careful of sharp exposed ends).
- Using three of the halves (discard the extra one), place the pieces together and twist in the centre to secure together.
- Splay the six ends out, so that you have a star shape.
- Thread six beads onto the end of each arm of the star, creating a pattern.
- Secure the beads by folding back the small piece of pipe cleaner that is left at each end and tucking into the centre hole of the end bead.

- If using a hanging thread, fasten onto the last unfolded pipe cleaner end and fold over as above to secure.

Variations:
Try an eight-sided star using all four pieces of the pipe cleaners.

Easier options:
Use 8mm faceted beads for smaller fingers.

ALL-AGE EXTRAS:
The magi faithfully followed the star, which led them to Jesus. How can our lives shine brightly, so that others are drawn to Jesus? Matthew 5:14–16 says: 'You are like light for the whole world. A city built on top of a hill cannot be hidden, and no one would light a lamp and put it under a clay pot. A lamp is placed on a lampstand, where it can give light to everyone in the house. Make your light shine, so that others will see the good that you do and will praise your Father in heaven.'

Use the star to remind you of how, each day, we can help others see Jesus, by the way we lead our lives. You could use each of the six arms on the star to remind you of six things that might help us each to shine better:

1 Don't hide your light.
2 Shine as a light in the world.
3 Follow the commandments God gave us.
4 Spend time talking and listening to God.
5 And reading his Word.
6 This will help us to grow the fruits of the Spirit – and SHINE!

BUTTON CROWN

Description: a collage crown of buttons and sequins
Difficulty level: ✽
Bible link: Matthew 2:1–12; Zechariah 9:16

YOU WILL NEED:
- A4 black card
- PVA glue or sticky glue dots
- variety yellow buttons
- gold sequin mix

INSTRUCTIONS
- Draw a simple three-pronged crown shape on black card.
- Use glue dots or PVA to cover the shape with buttons and sequins.

Variations:
Use different-coloured buttons or have each child create a different-coloured crown to display together.

Easier options:
Use sequins or stickers.

ALL-AGE EXTRAS:
Invite everyone to bring a button or circle of card to make up a large crown during the service. The magi recognised Jesus as King of the Jews, but many people did not. Jesus wasn't your normal type of king. He didn't wear a physical crown, except a crown of thorns on the cross. Jesus said he came as a servant King, which is not really what we expect from royalty. Everything in the Bible reflects this truth – his lowly birth, his entry into Jerusalem on a donkey, his profession as a carpenter, his life on the road amongst sinners – and yet Jesus is God's Son, King of the world. Is he king of our hearts? Do our lives shine like jewels in God's crown (Zechariah 9:16)?

PRINT & COLLAGE MAGI

Description: card with printed and collaged magi
Difficulty level: ✲ ✲
Bible link: Matthew 2:1–17

YOU WILL NEED:

- A4 white card folded to A5 landscape
- stencil cut from template (page 89)
- masking tape
- three paper plates
- sponge cut into pieces
- three different-coloured acrylic paints
- black fine liner pen
- skin-coloured paper
- gold-coloured paper or card
- large self-adhesive jewels
- small self-adhesive jewels and sequins

INSTRUCTIONS

- Cut stencil of magi bodies (page 89).
- Tape the stencil down on top of the white card.
- Squeeze one paint colour onto each paper plate.
- Using a small sponge, pick up the colour from one plate and dab through stencil (use hopping movements, do not wipe!) to create one magi body. Repeat with each colour.
- Carefully remove the stencil.
- Once dry, use semi-circular shapes for faces, and cut crowns from the gold paper to add to the top of the head.
- Use a fine liner to add simple arms and hands.
- Stick down jewels for the three gifts. Decorate the crowns with smaller jewels or sequins.

Variations:

Use a long sheet of paper and invite each child to create a figure (as above) that represents themselves. We can't bring Jesus costly jewels and gold, but can offer something far more valuable – ourselves.

Easier options:

Just use paper or craft foam collage shapes. Pre-cut for younger children.

ALL-AGE EXTRAS:

Let's look at two opposite reactions to Jesus being born.

How the magi reacted:
FIND the magi leave their homes to find Jesus
FAMILIAR with Scriptures
FORETOLD they know what has been foretold by the prophets
FOCUSED on what they had come for – to find Jesus and worship him
FAITHFULLY continue on their mission, despite Herod's attempts to thwart them
FOLLOWED the star, instructions from God in a dream
FELL at Jesus' feet in worship, offering gifts

How Herod reacted:
FEARFUL of the news the magi brought
FALSE COLOURS pretended he wanted to worship Jesus, when he didn't
FIBBED to obtain what he wanted
FURY at the escape of Jesus and the magi

How can our lives be more like those of the magi?

Three sparkling dramas that share the true story of Christmas. Suitable for use within a church service, at a community event or as stand-alone features.

A STORY IN SIX ACTS

This is a quiet, fairly straightforward retelling of the Christmas story. It is in six parts, so can be spread throughout a traditional service of carols and readings. The cast can be as big or small as you like, as the groups can be large, or actors can double up parts.

CAST

Narrator

Mary

An angel, with a group of other angels

Joseph

Some relatives of Joseph

Some shepherds

Simeon

Anna

Some wise men

Wise men's servants

King Herod

Some advisers of the king

A toddler Jesus

SETTING

The setting changes quite often, but no scenery is necessary. People can imagine where the characters are. You'll need some props (for example, a bed, a chair and a manger). If possible, use lights to highlight the angels – either from the ground or spotlights from above.

SCRIPT

1 THE GIRL WHO SAID YES

Narrator: Long ago, in the land of Israel, in the town of Nazareth, there lived a girl called Mary. *(Mary enters, carrying a mixing bowl and wooden spoon.)* Mary was engaged to a man called Joseph. One day, she received a surprise that would change her life, and the lives of everyone in the whole world.

An angel appears before Mary. Mary is so shocked that she drops her bowl and spoon.

Angel: You are truly blessed! The Lord is with you.
Mary: *(Confused.)* What? Who? I don't know what you mean!

Angel: Don't be afraid! God is pleased with you and you will have a son. His name will be Jesus. He will be great and will be called the Son of God Most High. The Lord God will make him king, as his ancestor David was. He will rule the people of Israel for ever, and his kingdom will never end.
Mary: *(Still confused.)* But how? I'm not married!
Angel: The Holy Spirit will come down to you, and God's power will come over you. So your child will be called the holy Son of God. Nothing is impossible for God! *(The angel leaves.)*
Mary: I am the Lord's servant. I will play my part in his plan.
Narrator: And so the angel left Mary. But what would Mary's future husband do when he found out about the baby?

They both exit.

2 THE MAN WHO CAME THROUGH

Narrator: In another part of Nazareth, a man was deeply troubled. *(Joseph enters.)*
Joseph: *(Speaking to himself.)* I can't believe she could do that to me. She's having a baby and it's not mine! What am I going to do? I know, I'll call the wedding off quietly. She doesn't deserve all that public humiliation, despite what she's done.

Joseph lies down on the floor (or on a bed, if you have one). An angel appears.

Angel: Joseph, the baby that Mary will have is from the Holy Spirit. Go ahead and marry her. Then after her baby is born, name him Jesus, because he will save his people from their sins.

The angel leaves. Joseph tosses and turns in his bed. Then he gets up.

Joseph: A baby from the Holy Spirit! Mary was telling the truth! I will marry her. I will play my part in God's plan. *(He exits.)*
Narrator: Joseph and Mary were married, just as the angel had told Joseph.

The narrator exits.

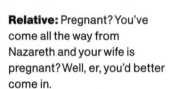

3 THE BABY WHO WAS BORN TO SAVE

Narrator: When Augustus was Roman Emperor, he ordered a census to be taken, so that he could list everyone for taxes. Each person had to go back to their home town to be counted. Joseph had to return to Bethlehem, the ancient home of his family, the family of King David.

Joseph and Mary enter. Mary is pregnant; Joseph is carrying a bag. A doll, wrapped in a blanket ,should be concealed in the bag.

Joseph: We're close now, Mary. Look, there is my family's house.

Joseph leaves Mary and the bag and goes to knock on the door (he can mime if you have no scenery). One of his relatives opens the door.

Relative: Yes? What can I do for you?
Joseph: My name is Joseph, I'm from the family of King David, but I live in Nazareth. I've come for the census.
Relative: Oh! Joseph! I'm afraid our guest room is full. We have had so many members of the family arrive, they've taken every bed we've got.
Joseph: *(Shocked.)* But my wife, Mary, is pregnant – we need somewhere to stay! You must have somewhere we can go!

Relative: Pregnant? You've come all the way from Nazareth and your wife is pregnant? Well, er, you'd better come in.

Joseph goes back to Mary and helps her into the house.

Relative: I suppose we can find some space over there. It's close to where the animals live, but it's the best I can do.
Joseph: Really? Are there no spare beds?
Mary: Joseph, it's warm and dry – it'll be fine. Remember what the angel said. *(She sits down.)*
Joseph: Yes. Fine. *(To the relative.)* Thank you.

Joseph and the relative stand in front of Mary. As she is shielded from view, she removes her pregnancy bump and gets the doll out of the bag.

Narrator: And soon it came time for Mary to have her baby.

Joseph and the relative part and Mary stands, carrying the baby in the blanket, and places the baby in the manger.

Narrator: Jesus was born, and they laid him in a manger, because that was all the room there was left.

After a pause, everyone leaves the stage, leaving Jesus in the manger.

4 THE WATCHERS WHO SAW

Narrator: That same night, on the hills above Bethlehem, some shepherds were watching their sheep. *(They enter and gather on one side of the stage.)* They too would get a wonderful surprise.

An angel appears in front of them.

Angel: Don't be afraid! I have good news for you, which will make everyone happy. This very day in King David's hometown a Saviour was born for you. He is Christ the Lord. You will know who he is, because you will find him dressed in baby clothes and lying on a bed of hay.

More angels appear behind the first one. Mary and Joseph come back on at the same time and stand behind the manger.

All the angels: Praise God in heaven! Peace on earth to everyone who pleases God!
Narrator: The shepherds rushed to the town to find the Saviour they'd been told about. They came to the house of Joseph's family and rushed inside. *(As the narrator says this, the shepherds do what is described.)*
Shepherd 1: It's true!
Shepherd 2: Those angels were right!
Mary: Angels?
Shepherd 3: Come on! We've got to tell everyone!

They rush off, chattering excitedly.

Mary: *(To Joseph.)* They said angels had told them about Jesus!

They all exit, taking Jesus with them.

5 THE ONES WHO WAITED

Narrator: In Jerusalem, there were two people waiting for Jesus. *(Simeon and Anna enter.)* They did not know about Mary and Joseph's son, but they knew God would soon send his Saviour.

Mary and Joseph enter, carrying the doll Jesus. Simeon rushes up to them.

Simeon: God told me I would see his Saviour and here you are! *(He takes the baby from Mary.)* O Lord! With my own eyes I have seen what you have done to save your people. Your mighty power is a light for all nations!

Simeon gives the baby back to Mary and leaves, singing and dancing. Anna rushes toward Mary and Joseph.

Anna: Look! It's the baby sent to save! Everyone see! I have been worshipping God in the Temple for decades and now I have seen the one sent to save us!

Anna rushes off stage, singing and dancing.

Narrator: Mary and Joseph wondered what had happened. They were really playing their part in God's plan.

They exit.

6 THE SAGES WHO TRAVELLED

Narrator: Far in the east, wise men were watching the skies. *(The wise men and their party enter.)* Suddenly they saw a star that caught their eye.

Wise man 1: Look! That star there. It's new!

Wise man 2: What do you mean?

Wise man 1: Just look! Surely that means something special has happened!

Wise man 2: You're right. That's the star of a king! We've got to find him!

Narrator: The wise men travelled a long way and finally came to the city of Jerusalem. They visited the palace of King Herod.

Herod and his advisers enter. The wise men and their party go to meet him.

Wise man 1: Where is the child born to be king of the Jews?

Wise man 2: We saw his star in the east and have come to worship him.

Narrator: Herod was worried – he was king of the Jews! He asked his advisers what they were talking about.

Herod: *(To his advisers.)* Where will the Messiah, God's special Saviour, be born?

Adviser 1: In Bethlehem, in the land of Judea.

Herod: *(To the wise men.)* Go to Bethlehem and search carefully for the child. As soon as you find him, let me know. I want to go and worship him too.

Narrator: The wise men travelled to Bethlehem and found the house where Jesus, Mary and Joseph lived.

Mary, Joseph and the toddler Jesus enter to be met by the wise men. They kneel before the family.

Wise man 1: *(Giving the gift to Joseph.)* Here is a gift of gold.

Wise man 2: *(Giving the gift to Mary.)* Here is a gift of frankincense.

Wise man 1: *(Giving the gift to Jesus.)* Here is a gift of myrrh.

Narrator: The wise men left, but went home without going back to Herod, because they had been warned not to do so in a dream.

The wise men leave in one direction, the family in the other.

GROWN-UP NATIVITY

This drama is a spoof nativity, where adults or young people play young children.

CAST
Mel, Naomi, Rachel, Tim, Mark, Rick, Matt, Zoe, Adam – school children in the nativity play

Mrs Rogerson – their teacher

SETTING
The setting is the stage of a primary school nativity play. There are some rudimentary pieces of set: a wonky stable, a palm tree and some toy sheep around a green bean bag. Mrs Rogerson should sit on the front row of the audience. A doll wrapped in a blanket should be hidden in the stable.

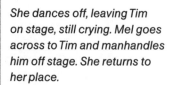

SCRIPT

Mel comes on stage, holding a scroll. She unrolls the scroll and starts reading from it in a monotonous voice.

Mel: A long time ago, in the town of Nazareth in the land of Israel, something special was about to happen. A girl called Mary was about to get a surprise.

There is a pause. Mel looks around nervously. She repeats her line loudly, looking off stage.

Mel: A girl called Mary was about to get a surprise.

There is some noise off stage, which develops into squabbling.

Mrs Rogerson: *(In a stage whisper.)* Naomi! Rachel! What's wrong!

Rachel and Naomi both shout from off stage.

Rachel: She won't give it me back!
Naomi: Give me back my mixing bowl!
Rachel: I haven't got your stupid mixing bowl. Tim's got it. See? Now give me my halo!
Naomi: Tim! Give it me back, bog-breath!

There is the sound of a scuffle, followed by the sound of Tim crying. Naomi marches on stage looking pleased with herself. She is dressed as Mary, holding the mixing bowl triumphantly in front of her, as well as a wooden spoon. Naomi overacts everything she does. She sits in the middle of the stage.

Naomi: *(Dramatically wiping her brow.)* Oh, I have so much work to do. I have swept the whole house and now I am making some delicious cakes for my fian… fia… financier, Joseph.

Rachel dances onto stage, using some cod-ballet moves. She is dressed as an angel, but her halo is wonky.

Rachel: *(In a dreamy voice.)* Behold! I am an angel! I have a message for…
Naomi: *(Interrupting.)* And then I have to wash clothes and feed the animals. Oh, it's so tiring. *(She stirs her bowl.)*
Rachel: *(Glaring at Naomi, but just maintaining her angelic poise.)* Behold! I am an angel! I have a mess…
Naomi: *(Interrupting again.)* After that I have to go to market to get some vegetables, and then visit Joseph…
Rachel: *(Losing her poise and shouting at Naomi. She moves closer and closer to Naomi, ending up shouting 'Afraid' in her face.)* Shut up! Shut up! Shut up! Shut up! I AM AN ANGEL AND I HAVE A MESSAGE FOR YOU! DO NOT BE AFRAAAAAAAAAAID!
Mrs Rogerson: *(In a stage whisper.)* Rachel!
Rachel: *(To Mrs Rogerson.)* But she wouldn't stop talking.
Mrs Rogerson: *(In a stage whisper.)* Well, just get on with it. And remember you're an angel, not a football hooligan.

Rachel rearranges herself. Naomi sticks her tongue out at her.

Rachel: You are going to have a baby.
Naomi: *(Giggling at this.)* But how? I'm not married!
Rachel: He will be God's Son. You will call him Jesus and he will reign for ever!

Mark appears, dressed as a king, holding an ostentatiously wrapped present.

Mark: Is it me yet?
Mrs Rogerson: No Mark! Not yet! Get back off stage!

He leaves sadly.

Mel: *(Reading again from her scroll.)* In another house in Nazareth, someone else was going to get a visitor.

Tim enters and tries to go to sleep, but Naomi is still on stage. He tries to push her out of the way, but she hits him with her wooden spoon.

Tim: Ow! *(He starts to cry again.)*
Mrs Rogerson: *(In a stage whisper.)* Naomi! *(She gets up and marches on stage. She wrestles the wooden spoon from Naomi's grasp.)* Get off stage!

Mrs Rogerson sits down again. Naomi slumps off stage in a huff. Tim is still crying.

Rachel: *(Ignoring Tim's crying.)* Joseph! Mary's baby is God's Son. You should call him Jesus, because he will save people from their sins.

She dances off, leaving Tim on stage, still crying. Mel goes across to Tim and manhandles him off stage. She returns to her place.

Mel: The Roman emperor decided that he wanted to know how many people there were in the empire. So he ordered that everyone go back to their home town. Joseph and Mary had to go to Bethlehem. So they packed up and set off.

Mark appears again, still holding his present.

Mark: Is it me now?
Mrs Rogerson: No Mark! Later! Later!

He leaves sadly. Tim and Naomi appear on stage. Naomi has a cushion underneath her costume and is sitting on Rick's back – Rick is on all fours, being the donkey.

Naomi: *(Kicking Rick on the side.)* Faster, donkey, faster! Joseph, if you really loved me, you'd get me a race horse, not this stupid donkey.

She kicks Rick again. Rick gets up, causing Naomi to topple off. If possible, her cushion should fall out.

Rick: I'm not being kicked for no one. *(He marches off.)*
Naomi: *(Trying to recover her cool.)* Joseph! Help me up! *(She retrieves her cushion and shoves it back into her costume.)*
Mel: When they got to Bethlehem, there was nowhere to stay, but they found some space where the animals lived.

They stop at the stable and sit down in front of it.

Naomi: Joseph! Why didn't you book ahead? I told you a million times to call your family. But no! You were 'too busy'! Now we have to stay with these stinky animals. I should have listened to my mother.
Mrs Rogerson: *(In a stage whisper.)* Naomi! Stop making the lines up!
Mel: And it came time for Mary to have her baby.

Naomi swoons and lies on the floor facing away from the audience. She immediately stands up again, holding the doll that was hidden in the stable.

Naomi: Phew! That was hard work.

Naomi cuddles her baby, Tim looks cowed next to her. Meanwhile, Rick, Matt and Zoe walk on, and stand on and around the green bean bag. They are carrying toy sheep and walking-stick crooks. Zoe wears a fake beard.

Mel: In the hills above Bethlehem, some shepherds were looking after their sheep.

Mark appears again, holding his present.

Mark: It's got to be my turn now!

Mrs Rogerson: *(With her head in her hands.)* No. Not now, Mark.

He leaves sadly. Mel, unsure of what to do, repeats her line.

Mel: Er, in the hills above Bethlehem, some shepherds were looking after their sheep.
Rick: Oh, it's hard work, looking after these sheep.

Matt stares at the audience in fear.

Rick: *(Repeating his line looking pointedly at Matt.)* I said it's hard work, looking after these sheep.

Matt continues to stare at the audience in fear.

Zoe: *(Putting her ear to Matt's mouth.)* What's that you say Matt? You agree that it's hard work? Ooh, I know. My feet are killing me. *(She suddenly remembers she's meant to be a man and starts to speak in a low 'male' voice.)* I can't wait to get home.

Adam appears, dressed as an angel.

Adam: Don't be afraid! I have good news for you!

Rachel rushes on and pushes Adam out of the way.

Rachel: Hey! That's my line! I'm the top angel! *(Holding off Adam with one hand.)* Don't be afraid! I have good news for you!

Adam pushes back. During their next lines they jostle for position. Rick and Zoe watch, bemused. Matt continues to stare at the audience.

Adam: Today in King David's home town…
Rachel: …home town a Saviour was born for you…
Adam: …for you. He is Christ the Lord…
Rachel: …the Lord. You will know…
Adam: …know who he is…
Rachel: *(Quickly, so she can get everything in before Adam interrupts again.)* …because you will find him dressed in baby clothes and lying on a bed of hay!
Mrs Rogerson: *(Getting up, muttering to herself.)* I should have been a prison warden, it would have been easier. *(She stands between Adam and Rachel, holding each one by the arm.)* Come on, say the next line together.
Rachel and Adam: *(In a huff, monotonously.)* Praise-God-in-heaven-Peace-on-earth-to-everyone-who-pleases-God.
Mrs Rogerson: Now go and sit down.

Rachel and Adam walk off the front of stage and walk down an aisle, instead of going off into the wings. They push and shove each other as they go.

Mrs Rogerson: *(Calling after them.)* No, not down the aisle! Oh, it doesn't matter. *(She sits down on the front row again.)*
Zoe: *(In her own voice.)* Come on! *(In her 'male' voice.)* Let's go and find him!

Rick and Zoe run to the stable. Matt continues to stare at the audience until Rick goes back and drags him by the hand to the stable.

Rick: We have heard about the birth of the Saviour and we have come to worship him.
Zoe: Here. Have a sheep. *(She throws a toy sheep at Tim.)*
Rick: Come on, let's tell everyone about Jesus!

Rick and Zoe start to go off stage, realise Matt's not with them and return to drag him off stage. Mark comes on.

Mark: It has to be me now!
Mrs Rogerson: It may as well be. Come on, then, say your lines.

Mark opens his mouth and then forgets what he's meant to say. He bursts into tears, drops his present and runs off stage. Naomi and Tim go off, Naomi berating Tim as she leaves. Mel looks frantically at her scroll to see what she should say next. Eventually she looks at the very bottom of her scroll.

Mel: And that's the story of Jesus' birth.

NO ROOM

This drama is mostly a monologue by a relative of Joseph's. It can be performed by a man or a woman, with the character's name being Judah or Judith. The other characters enter to give Judah/Judith bits of news.

CAST

Judah/Judith – a relative of Joseph's who runs the household

Ruth – Judah/Judith's daughter

Joseph

Simeon – Judah/Judith's son

SETTING

The drama is set in the house of Joseph's relatives, in Bethlehem. You need one chair, but you could have some simple tables and more chairs to set the household scene.

SCRIPT

Judah/Judith: (Noticing and then addressing the audience.) More house guests! You can't want a place to sleep – I've not got enough room for one more person, never mind all you lot! Honestly, it's been like Piccadilly Circus in here! If Piccadilly Circus actually existed yet… Relatives have been arriving non-stop for the last three weeks. It's that stupid Emperor's fault, wanting to know how many people there were, so he can tax them. Everyone has had to return to their home town and, for my family, that means coming here to Bethlehem. I've got people staying here that I've never even met before!

We've got cousins and distant relatives in the guest room – most of whom have done nothing but criticise since they got here. (Judah/Judith mimics his/her relatives.) 'Ooh, isn't your house small?' 'I wouldn't have put the bed there.' 'Are you letting your children go out at this time?' I can't wait to see the back of

them. Fresh fish and visitors stink after three days. All my immediate family are in the main living quarters, and blow me down if a fella called Joseph doesn't turn up the other night with his pregnant wife. Turns out he's from part of the family that now lives in Nazareth, about 70 miles away! There was no space anywhere. They had to find some room in between the kitchen and where the animals live. I feel a bit sorry for them, but they seem to be OK. I think they have had a tough time of it in Nazareth. Joseph didn't say very much, but some of the family said they'd heard rumours (Judah/Judith lowers his/her voice to a stage whisper) that Mary was pregnant before they got married. (Back to a normal voice.) Still, not my place to judge. And I couldn't see them out in the street, could I?

Ruth enters.

Judah/Judith: (To Ruth.) What? Don't tell me more people have arrived!
Ruth: No, nothing like that. Well actually, it might be.
Judah/Judith: What do you mean?
Ruth: It's Mary, Joseph's wife. She's gone into labour. I think the baby is going to be born soon!
Judah/Judith: (Running about the place in a panic.) Quick! Quick! Get hot water! Towels! Call the midwife!
Ruth: It's OK, Auntie Hannah and Auntie Deborah have sorted everything out. You might need to help Joseph, though, he's gone a weird shade of green.
Judah/Judith: (Calming down.) Right, yes. Go and get him and we'll help him feel a bit better.

Ruth exits.

Judah/Judith: Wow! A baby, born here! That hasn't happened for a few years. I remember when my son, Reuben, was born. I thought my dad was going to keel over! It was wonderful though. The joy of a new life coming into the world… Mind you, a new life coming into the world is another mouth to feed and person to look after. And worry about. You never stop worrying about your family, no matter how old they get.

Ruth enters with Joseph and guides him to a chair.

Ruth: There you go, Joseph, sit there and I'll get you a drink. (She gets a cup and fills it with water from a jug. She gives it to him.)

Judah/Judith mimes to Ruth, asking her if Joseph is OK. Ruth mimes back that he's not!

Ruth: I'll come back in a bit, Joseph, and let you know how things are getting on.

She exits. Judah/Judith approaches Joseph tentatively.

Judah/Judith: So… Joseph… Holding up?
Joseph: (Taking a deep breath.) I'll be OK. It all happened a bit suddenly, that's all.
Judah/Judith: Don't worry! When Ruth was born, it was fairly straightforward. Mind you, Simeon was a different kettle of fish. He took so long that my wife/I had to walk around the courtyard for ages, waiting for him to come. I thought it would never happen. (Notices Joseph looking worried.) Oh… I'm sure that won't happen for Mary though. It's a bit of a nuisance you having to travel here for the census.

Joseph: Yes, well… It was a bit awkward in Nazareth. You know what it's like in a small town like that. So many people seem to know your business. And our business is surprising to say the least. I was secretly glad to get away.
Judah/Judith: What do you mean?
Joseph: Well, Mary fell pregnant before we got married and… the baby isn't actually mine.
Judah/Judith: What?! Why did you marry her? She cheated on you – didn't that matter?
Joseph: It's not as simple as that…
Judah/Judith: I think it is! She treated you like mud! I'm not surprised Nazareth was difficult for you! Only an idiot would have married Mary!
Joseph: No! Wait a minute! (He pauses.) Listen, what I'm about to tell you sounds impossible, but… well, nothing's impossible for God, is it?
Judah/Judith: Go on.
Joseph: The baby will be God's Son, God's promised Saviour.

Judah/Judith laughs loudly at this, but soon stops when he/she sees Joseph's serious face.

Judah/Judith: What? You're being serious?
Joseph: Yes. Mary was visited by an angel. He told her that she was going to have a baby and it would be conceived by the Holy Spirit. She, of course, was shocked, but the angel reminded her that her cousin Elizabeth was way too old to have a baby, but she was pregnant. So Mary said she would do what God asked.
Judah/Judith: She told you that and you believed her?
Joseph: Not at first. I was all ready to call the wedding off. I was going to do it quietly – Mary's a wonderful girl and even if she'd made a mistake, I didn't want to shame her publicly. But then I had a dream.
Judah/Judith: We all have dreams! I once dreamt that I was face to face with a mountain bear and all I had to fight him off was a mouse, a loaf of bread and a seven-branched candlestick!
Joseph: It wasn't really a dream, more of a vision. An angel came to me in a dream and told me to marry Mary, that the baby was from God and was going to be the Messiah, God's chosen Saviour.
Judah/Judith: But Joseph, that was just a dream.
Joseph: Oh, Judah/Judith, it was so much more than that. The angel, the feeling of God's love and glory, the stunning sight. It was real. A holy and awe-inspiring visit from God's messenger!
Judah/Judith: (Doubtfully.) I suppose it could have been.

Ruth rushes on excitedly.

Ruth: Joseph! Joseph! He's here! The baby's arrived!
Judah/Judith: Already? That was quick!
Ruth: Come on! You've got to see!

Ruth grabs Joseph by the hand and drags him off.

Ruth: (Exiting.) We've had to put him in a feeding trough, but we cleared it out first!
Judah/Judith: (Putting his/her hand to his/her forehead.) Already! The baby's here. (Turning to the audience.) Do you believe that story of Joseph's? That the baby is from God? It seems all a bit far-fetched to me.

Simeon runs on from the opposite side of the stage.

Simeon: Dad/Mum! There are three shepherds at the door!
Judah/Judith: Shepherds? What do they want? Simeon, tell them we're full. No room, no food, no place for them at all. I'm not having shepherds in my house. Some of us have got standards you know!
Simeon: They say they've come to see the baby born to be God's special Saviour.
Judah/Judith: (Shocked.) What did you say? A baby? God's special Saviour?
Simeon: Yes. Get this, they say that an angel told them about the boy. And then a whole host, a gang, a choir of angels appeared and started singing a heavenly song!
Judah/Judith: (Even more shocked.) Angels? They were sent here by angels?
Simeon: Er, that's what they said.

Judah/Judith is dumbfounded.

Simeon: Dad/Mum? Should I get rid of them?
Judah/Judith: (Slowly, trying to take it in.) No, let them in.

Simeon disappears leaving Judah/Judith with his/her mouth wide open in disbelief. He returns, leading three shepherds across the stage, all chattering excitedly about angels, Saviours and abandoned sheep. As they pass Judah/Judith, he/she points them in the right direction, still open-mouthed. After they have gone, Judah/Judith slowly sits on a chair.

Judah/Judith: Somebody pinch me. When Joseph told me that story, I thought Mary had really taken him for a ride. But now… could it be real? Could the Messiah, the one we've all been waiting for, really be in my house? Now? As a baby?

Ruth reappears at the side of the stage.

Ruth: Dad/Mum! What are you waiting for? Come and meet the baby! Come and meet Jesus!

Ruth leaves. Judah/Judith stands up and looks at where she has just gone. He/she turns to look at the audience, and waves uncertainly.

Judah/Judith: Right. Er, help yourself to whatever you want. I'm off to see the Saviour of the world.

He/she hurries off.

These games are designed to fit into your Christmas activities. Choose one or more according to your aims, space, time and resources available. They are grouped into party, active, relay and sit-down games, but many of them can form part of a party or family fun day.

Make sure you risk assess each activity so that everyone is kept as safe as possible.

GAMES

PARTY GAMES

Children (and adults!) enjoy several Christmas parties each year, but their enthusiasm for another one is rarely blunted! Here are three party games, together with some suggestions of what else you might do.

SPLITTING PASS THE PARCEL

What you need: eight identical prizes, newspaper or wrapping paper, scissors, sticky tape, music and the means to play it, wrapped sweets (optional)

Before the session, wrap up the eight prizes. Then group these together in pairs and wrap each pair up. Pair these four parcels up and wrap the pairs to make two parcels. Wrap these two up together to make one parcel. To make the game longer, you can include extra layers of wrapping at each of the stages.

Start the game as you would a normal Pass the Parcel. When someone opens the parcel to find two packages inside, send each parcel opposite ways round the circle. Keep this going until the eight prizes are unwrapped.

You can change the number of prizes according to the number of people you have; starting 12 or 16 prizes will fit the format of pairing and wrapping. You could also include a sweet in each layer.

For a story-based game, break down the Christmas story into the same number of parts as you have layers. Write out each part of the story on a separate slip of paper and then include one slip in each layer. At the end of the game, challenge everyone to put together the story in the right order.

CHRISTMAS FOOD TASTING

What you need: blindfolds, a selection of Christmas food (such as Christmas pudding, tangerines, sprouts, turkey or gingerbread) (be aware of hygiene and allergy issues), spoons (enough for one per food per player), table and chairs

Before the session, source a selection of Christmas food and put each one into a closed container. Just before you play the game, set these out on a table, and put out enough chairs for your players to sit down.

Ask for some volunteers to play the game; make sure they are happy to be blindfolded and check for food allergies and any vegetarians or vegans. Explain that they are going to be tasting various Christmas food items – they should try to guess what they're eating. Play the game, showing the children who are not playing what you're going to feed your contestants – the audience reaction will add extra jeopardy for the players! Use a different spoon per contestant per food.

GAMES

DOUGHNUT GAME

What you need: ring doughnuts, string

Before the party, tie a length of string across a part of your room (if there's nothing you can use to tie up string, then something like badminton-net posts would be ideal). Tie a piece of string to each doughnut (threading it through the hole) and then hang the doughnuts at intervals on the long piece of string so that they hang down at head height (if you have a mix of ages playing, hang the doughnuts at different heights).

Invite players to stand in front of a hanging doughnut and place their hands behind their back. Give a signal for everyone to try to eat the doughnut off the string using only their mouths. The winner is the first one to finish.

Be aware of food hygiene and allergy issues, and you might want to put out a tablecloth on the floor under the doughnuts so that the children can eat their doughnut even if it comes off the string. For a biscuit version of this game, use Party Rings or make gingerbread circles with a hole in the middle (or maybe even gingerbread snowflakes!).

OTHER PARTY GAMES

There are lots of other traditional party games you might play. Musical games, such as chairs, bumps or statues are always popular (though be careful that musical chairs doesn't get too competitive!). Let your artistic side out and create a donkey and tail for Pin the Tail on the Donkey – or maybe you could pin the red nose on Rudolph! Rework Duck, Duck, Goose to fit a Christmas theme, maybe into Santa, Santa, Reindeer. Play Kim's Game with a tray of Christmas objects, such as a bauble, an angel, a star and a small present.

ACTIVE GAMES

SNOWBALL FIGHT

What you need: newspaper, chalk or masking tape, timer

Before the session, scrunch up sheets of newspaper into balls to make snowballs, and mark a line down the middle of your space with chalk or masking tape. Split the group into two teams and position the teams on either side of the centre line. Scatter the snowballs equally on each side.

Challenge the teams to throw the snowballs onto their opponents' side of the room. Give the group a time limit and then shout 'Go!' This game will be frantic and furious, so have plenty of supervisors to make sure everyone stays safe and no one gets too competitive.

At the end of the time limit, count up how many snowballs are in each team's area – the one with the fewer is the winner!

PUDDING BALL

What you need: a brown ball (such as a basketball), two large pans, timer, whistle

Before the session, make your ball look like a Christmas pudding – you could paint some icing or custard on top of it and draw on black circles for raisins! Place a pan at each end of the playing space (make sure they are big enough for the ball to fit inside).

Split the group into two teams and send them each to a pan. Explain that they have to get the Christmas pudding (ball) into their opponents' pan, while stopping the opposition from doing the same. Lay out some rules – no contact allowed, no running with the pudding, no fighting over the pudding. Set a time limit on the game and make sure you referee the game fairly. The team that gets the pudding in their opponents' pan the most is the winner.

CHRISTMAS TREASURE HUNT

What you need: pictures of each of the Christmas story objects and people (see below), clues for your treasure hunt, prizes

Before the session, come up with some clues for a treasure hunt. Your clues should direct teams around your venue, to eight locations; at each location they will uncover an object or person to do with the Christmas story. Print out enough copies of each story object and person for each team to collect one as they go round.

1 Angel
2 Mary
3 Joseph
4 Roman Emperor
5 Baby Jesus
6 Sheep
7 Star
8 Gift

You can also place some wrapped sweets in each location for people to collect as they go round. Play this in teams or individually.

Once everyone has been to each of the locations and collected the pictures, challenge each group to retell the story of Christmas using the pictures they have collected. Give help to any individual or group that might need it. If you have a group of children participating in this game, invite them to retell the story to the rest of the group, if they wish.

RELAY GAMES

CHRISTMAS DINNER TRAY

What you need: one tray per team, play food and empty boxes to represent various parts of a Christmas dinner (for example, play carrots, rubber chickens, Christmas pudding boxes or basins, custard tins or cartons and strings of sausages made from tights and newspaper) – you'll need one complete meal per team, chalk or masking tape

Mark a start line using the chalk or masking tape. Split the group into teams and line them up behind the start line. Give the first person in each team a tray and place one of each of your Christmas dinner items at the other end of the space, opposite each team.

On the word 'Go!', the first person goes to the end of the room, puts an item on the tray and returns to their team. They give the tray and first item to the second person, who takes it to the end of the space to collect another item, and so on. The teams must keep all their items on the tray. If anything falls off, then that item is returned to the pile at the end and the team must collect it again. The winning team is the one that collects all their items first.

Make sure you risk assess this thoroughly, so that people are safe carrying the tray. You might want to outlaw running with the tray!

TREE DECORATING

What you need: lots of Christmas tree decorations in a big bucket, a Christmas tree for each team

Mark a start line using the chalk or masking tape. Split the group into teams and line them up behind the start line. Give each team a Christmas tree (try to make sure they're all the same size) and place your bucket of decorations at the other end of your space. The first team member has to run to the bucket, collect a decoration and return to their team. Then the next player goes, and so on. The team must use the decorations to make their trees as Christmassy as possible. (You may want to have more than one bucket of decorations if you have lots of teams, to avoid a crush!)

Once you have finished, judge which of the teams has decorated their tree the best!

OTHER RELAY IDEAS

There are lots of other relay races you can play. Cut up a Christmas picture into pieces. Players run in turn to collect a piece of the picture and then, when all the pieces have been collected, the team has to put together the Christmas scene. The first one to do so wins.

You could do the same with the Christmas story. Split the Christmas story into parts and write each part on a separate slip of paper. Teams have to collect the parts of the story and then put them all in the right order.

GAMES

SIT-DOWN GAMES

STICKY CHARACTERS

What you need: sticky notes, marker pen

Before the session, write out character names from the Christmas story, each on a separate sticky note. Try some of these: Mary, Joseph, Angel Gabriel, Emperor Augustus, Jesus, Shepherd, Herod, Wise man. If you have lots of people in your group, then add in some traditional Christmas names, such as Father Christmas or Rudolph.

Stick one sticky note to the forehead of each person in the group (without letting them see the name on their sticky note). Encourage everyone to ask yes/no questions to the others in the group to find out who their character is. Once someone has discovered their name, they can help others by answering their questions. If someone isn't happy about having a sticky note stuck to their forehead, then stick it to their back instead.

CHRISTMAS ANAGRAMS

What you need: the anagrams below printed out on paper (one per person) or from page 90, pens or pencils

Give each person a copy of the anagrams below. They are anagrams of Christmas words. Challenge them to be the first to finish!

SEJUS
RYAM
SPOJEH
HODER
BIRAGLE
HERPHEDS
SIWE NMA
RATS
TIMSCRASH
UBBEAL
STREPEN
GOCKINTS
LAWNSLOB
FAWNSLOKE

The answers are: Jesus, Mary, Joseph, Herod, Gabriel, shepherd, wise man, star, Christmas, bauble, present, stocking, snowball, snowflake

You could play this as a relay, with each player running to a leader, who gives them an anagram. They take this anagram back to their group, and the next person goes. While people are running, the rest of the team try to solve the anagrams. Depending on the age and ability of your group, you might choose to add some more challenging Christmas-themed words.

GUESS THE PRESENT

What you need: enough wrapped presents for each person to have one, gift tags, pencils

Before the session, buy enough small gifts for each person in your group to have one. Try to get gifts of equal value, but of different sizes and shapes (a pound shop is a good place to go). Wrap the gifts and attach a blank gift tag to each one.

Spread the gifts out in front of the group and ask them to pick one each. Explain that this is not a present for them to open! They should feel and rattle their present and try to guess what's in it. When they think they have an idea, they should write it on the gift tag, and put their name next to their guess. Then everyone should swap the gift with someone else and try to guess what this one is. Keep this going until each tag has three or four names and guesses on it, before placing the presents back in the middle.

Invite everyone now to choose a gift to open (but not keep). Do this one at a time, and then compare the guesses on the gift tag with the actual present. Award the present to the person whose guess was the closest, the funniest or maybe the worst! Keep opening and awarding the presents until you have finished. As you award the gifts, make sure that everyone ends up with something!

GAMES

CHRISTMAS BOARD GAME

What you need: copies of the game board from page 91, counters and dice

Split all the players into smaller groups. Give each group a copy of the game board, a dice and enough counters for everyone to have one each. Each group can play the game at their own pace. The first person to get to the end of the board is the winner. Once everyone has finished, use the game board to tell the Christmas story.

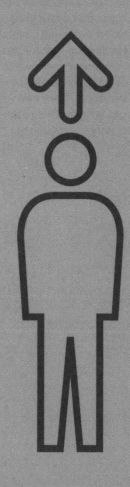

Twelve prayer activities to help people of all ages spend time with God this Christmas season. Talking and silence, walking and stillness, making and drawing – pray in many different ways as you go deeper into this well-known story.

PRAYERS

WORD BECAME FLESH

YOU WILL NEED:
play dough, a baby doll

This prayer activity helps us to begin to consider how wonderful and strange it is that God would come to us as a baby.

Give each person in the group a piece of play dough and ask them to fashion their play dough into something that represents how they see God. After some time, ask them to share what they've shaped. (To avoid making anyone uncomfortable you could ask, 'Who would like to share what they've made?' rather than assuming they will all want to share.) Enjoy a time of sharing people's ideas, and be affirming and interested.

Bring out the baby doll; ask whether anyone thought of this – imagining God as a baby. Invite the group to respond with their reactions.

Explain that at Christmas we celebrate God coming to us as a baby. Isn't that bizarre, when you think about it?! A baby is helpless, weak and completely dependent – something that we don't often put with our idea of God! Ask the group: 'What do you think it says about who God is, that he would come as a baby?' Encourage them to discuss.

Ask the group to put all of their play dough representations of God in the middle with the doll. Introduce a time of prayerful reflection by asking the group to silently consider how we see God, and what it meant for him to come to us as a baby. They can use the doll and the different play dough models as a way to help them reflect. To close this time of silence, read John 1:1–18 to the group. Pray a finishing prayer, thanking God for all the ways he reveals himself to us, and that we may continue to understand more of him as we celebrate the arrival of this baby to earth.

BRINGING LIGHT PRAYER WALK

YOU WILL NEED:

glow sticks and enough adult volunteers to supervise, and consent to leave the premises with children and/or young people

This activity is best done late afternoon or evening for full glow-stick effect!

Ask the group: 'If you didn't already know the Christmas story, and someone told you that God was planning to come to earth, what kinds of places do you think God would first arrive in?' Invite them to discuss.

Explain that what we know about where Jesus arrived is that he chose pretty much the most humble and unnoticeable spot to appear in – the back room of an inn. And yet, because he was the Son of God, he brought light to that small, humble and unnoticeable place!

Ask them to think about where the small, unnoticeable spots in their community are. If Jesus was to arrive and bring his light into places that other people might not take notice of, where would they be?

Explain that you are going on a prayer walk, to take Jesus' light into these places. (It is a good idea to plan a small, manageable route around the local area.)

Follow a route around the local area, and every time you reach a spot where the group would like to pray, stop and pray that Jesus would bring his light to that place (for example, outside a nursing home, near doctors' surgeries, in run-down buildings or places where people might be on their own). If you think that it might be difficult for your group to pray, you could simply pray, 'Jesus, may your light be known here' at each point. As a sign of praying for Jesus' light to enter a place, break a few glow sticks every time you stop. As you keep stopping and praying in different spots, you will have a gathering presence of light in the glow sticks, so that as you progress around your route you will be collectively carrying a lot of light with you.

When you finish and arrive back, allow the group members to take the glow sticks with them! They're fun to play with but may also be a good reminder of Jesus' light and the prayers they prayed.

WAITING IT OUT

YOU WILL NEED:
printed copies of the liturgy, Bibles or copies of Luke 2:22–40

Together, read out Luke 2:22–40. In this story Jesus is presented as a baby at the Temple. Two significant characters are introduced; Simeon and Anna, both deeply faithful people who were waiting to meet Jesus before they died. They knew that God was going to send the Messiah, and had waited faithfully for many years. We read that when Simeon and Anna meet the baby Jesus, they give thanks to God. This is an example of extraordinary faith. It is difficult to wait for things we are desperate for, and Anna and Simeon waited such a long time before they saw their hope realised in Jesus.

Ask the group to think for a moment: Is there anything that they are hoping for or waiting for? Give the group some time to consider this. After a while, allow the group to share any of the things they were thinking of. Then pray this liturgy together.

Jesus, thank you for those who watched and waited for you
And thank you that you came.

Thank you that, though the years passed, they kept their faith in you
And thank you that you still came.

Jesus, when we wait
Help us keep our faith in you.

Jesus, when we wait
Help us keep our hope in you.

Jesus, though we are young
Keep our faith strong through to when we are old.

Jesus, we give you the things we wait for:
Our hopes and dreams,
Our ambitions and futures,
The things you have promised us
And the things we don't know if you want us to have.
We place them all into your hands.
We don't know what the future holds,
But we know you are good.
We know that you promised you would come to us,
And you did.
You gave Anna and Simeon hope two thousand years ago.
Please give us hope today
And the strength to keep on hoping.
Amen.

GIFTS FOR JESUS

YOU WILL NEED:

a wrapped-up present, present tags, pens, sticky tape, worship music

At Christmas we often think about Jesus as a gift to us. He was the Son of God, given to us as a lavish gift, as the one who would show us the way back to God, and ultimately die so that we may be with God for eternity.

But what about the idea of giving Jesus gifts? Ask the group if they can remember what Jesus was given by his visitors at his birth. In Matthew 2 we read about the magi giving gold, frankincense and myrrh. These are thought to have particular significance because of their symbolism: gold to signify that Jesus was a king, frankincense to show that Jesus had a priestly role and myrrh (which was used in burial and embalming) to show that Jesus was born to die.

Discuss with the group what kinds of gifts Jesus would want us to give him today. Does he want things, or does he want attitudes or commitments of different things, such as time or relationships or careers? Talk together about this.

Have a symbolic present wrapped and ready. You could use a cardboard box so that it's a big visual display, wrapped and with bows on. Have a pile of gift tags and pens ready.

Explain to the group that this present represents a present that we're going to give to Jesus. Invite everyone to take as many tags as they wish and to write down things that they want to pledge as gifts to Jesus. Their gifts might include time, objects, plans, hopes or something different. Give the group enough time to write their tags and then to stick them onto the present as a sign that they are committing these gifts to Jesus. You could play some worship music so that there is an atmosphere of praise. At the end, pray for the group, or pray together.

You might like to use the following words:

Jesus, you are the greatest gift of all time, thank you. Thank you that you love us and that we can give our own humble gifts to you. We pray that these will bless you. Amen.

PRAYERS FOR REFUGEES AT CHRISTMAS

YOU WILL NEED:

card, scissors, glue,newspaper clippings about refugees (it might be a good idea to ask friends who get a newspaper to look out and keep relevant news stories a few weeks before; alternatively, you could try refugee charity websites (such as Refugee Action) that profile stories of refugees)

Read the group the following story:

A young couple are away from home when their baby is born. Homeless, they are given a back room somewhere out of the way for her to give birth. Before they can even get their stuff together, get sorted and find somewhere else to stay, they find out that they and their baby son are in danger. The only chance of keeping him safe is to go far away, somewhere even more unstable, where they don't speak the language or know the customs. With hardly anything to call their own, this barely formed family is on the run. They end up in Egypt, alone but at least with each other and their lives, Israeli refugees.

Ask them: Who is this about? What do you know about the story of Mary and Joseph fleeing Bethlehem with the very young baby Jesus? Explain that we can read more about this in Matthew 2.

Say: This means Jesus himself was a refugee. It's amazing that God, who made the world, could become a vulnerable refugee child. This is an example of how Jesus, from the start, identified with the least powerful and most vulnerable among us.

Spread out different stories about refugees and ask the group to read them. Ask each group member to choose a story that they want to pray for over Christmas, as they remember how Jesus, too, was a refugee. Encourage each person to cut out their story and mount it on card, so that they can keep it somewhere prominent that will remind them to pray. Discuss with the groups the kinds of things they could pray for.

As a group, spend some time praying for refugees. Invite them to pray for the refugees in the stories they have chosen, as well as those in any other current stories.

PRAYERS **06**

NATIVITY PRAYERS

YOU WILL NEED:
a nativity set, pens and paper

If you don't have a nativity set, it's likely that someone in your church will have one. So ask around!

Set out the nativity set. As you put it together, chat with the group about the nativity story using the different characters.*

Split the group into twos or threes. Give each small group a figure from the nativity (eg a shepherd, an angel), a pen and some paper. Ask them to write Christmas prayers from the perspective of their character. Encourage them to think about what Christmas meant to them, how they saw Jesus, how playing their part in the Christmas story may have changed them, what we can learn from them.

Give them some time and space to write out their prayers.

When they're ready, ask everyone to come back together with their characters. Ask someone from each small group to lead the rest of you in prayer with the prayer they've written from their character's perspective. Once they've prayed, invite them to put their figure back in place in the nativity scene. Keep going until the nativity set is complete again and every group has read their prayer.

*For a bit of fun, you could show a really great version of the nativity story acted out by St Paul's Church, Auckland, New Zealand. It's very well made and is available on YouTube, called The Christmas Story by stpaulsartandmedia. (Note the restrictions given in the text underneath the clip.)

ADVENT AND ANTICIPATION

YOU WILL NEED:

blank Advent calendars. (either find a copyright-free template online to print off or buy ready-made craft templates online), Advent candles (the long ones with a countdown on the side), pens

Ask the group what they know about Advent. Why is it an important part of Christmas? Discuss as a group.

Explain that the word 'Advent' is derived from the Latin 'to come', and Advent is all about waiting for the coming birth of Jesus. Sometimes the build-up to Christmas can be the best part, but sometimes it's easy to forget that the celebration and excitement are really all about the most amazing thing – Jesus' birth!

Advent is meant to help us to focus on what we're waiting for, and keeps Jesus' coming central to Christmas.

Introduce the Advent calendars and candles – give one to everyone. Explain that these are going to be used as tools to help us pray and focus on awaiting Jesus' birth!

Say that Advent candles are meant to be lit for a short period every day, burning down through the numbers on the side as Christmas Day gets closer. Remind your group that the Advent candle also reminds us to take some time to pray each day as we wait for Jesus.

Explain that the blank Advent calendar is ready to be filled in, with something written in each day to pray about – such as people who may find Christmas hard, things to give thanks for about Jesus or aspects of Christmas to pray or reflect on. Invite everyone to take a pen and fill in their Advent prayer calendar. Give them some time to do this. You might like to play some appropriate music in the background during this time. Afterwards, invite the group to share a few of the things they've written on their calendars.

Finish the session by praying that the calendars and candles would be a helpful way of us spending time with God and awaiting Christmas Day.

BLEAK MIDWINTER KITS

YOU WILL NEED:

items for creating hot chocolate kits, Christmas cards, pens

This is a way of praying and caring for people who may be finding Christmas difficult. You will put together 'Bleak Midwinter Kits' so that everyone can take one to someone else to warm them through the winter – spiritually and literally!

Gather together things that will make a nice hot chocolate kit – small hot chocolate sachets, marshmallows, chocolate bars. You could make these kits particularly fancy by buying plain mugs and ceramic pens, and encouraging your group to create custom mugs. Obviously, this will increase the budget and time this activity will take. Alternatively, you could get some plain paper bags that could be drawn or written on. Other things like tissue paper, cellophane and ribbons will make these kits even lovelier gifts to give.

Get creative about other things that could be added to the bag: maybe candles or warm socks!

Explain to the group that Christmas can be tricky for some people. They might have too much on, they might be lonely or have family difficulties, they might be sick or find it hard to get out, or they may just loathe the cold! Outline your plan, maybe showing a sample kit, then ask each member of the group to choose someone who may need a little more love this Christmas.

Give out Christmas cards and explain that these will go with the packages. Give everyone time to think about what they want to say: Can they write a prayer for this person? Would it be better to just tell them that they are praying for them this Christmas? Can they write a letter that is supportive and affirming and lets the recipient know they are thinking of them?

Give the group some time to write their cards and then gather everyone to pray for the recipients. You could give space for everyone to pray out loud, or you could say a prayer and give everyone a space to name the people their kits are going to!

Then spend some time making your kits together.

THANK-YOU LETTER PRAYERS

YOU WILL NEED:

letter paper, envelopes and pens

At Christmas we spend a lot of time thinking about presents – what we'll get other people and what we might ask for! We try to choose the best gift for the people we know, and we spend quite a bit of time thinking about what we really need or want as we ask for things.

John 3:16 is a very well-known Bible verse that says: 'God loved the people of this world so much that he gave his only Son, so that everyone who has faith in him will have eternal life and never really die.'

This passage explains who Jesus is and that God sent him to save us. Through Jesus we are freely given relationship with God, the promises of eternal life and hope for the future. In short, Jesus is pretty much the best Christmas present we could ever be given.

In the tradition of Christmas, when we're given presents we write thank-you letters in response to our gifts (often only at the encouragement of parents!). It's a chance to thank people for their generosity and tell them what their gift means to us.

Explain that today there will be the opportunity to write thank-you letter prayers to God, thanking him for the gift of Jesus.

Give everyone a pen, some letter paper and an envelope, and invite them to write a thank-you letter to God. Encourage them to elaborate on their thank you in the following ways:

- what does being given the gift of Jesus mean to them?
- what difference does Jesus make in their lives?
- how does knowing Jesus chose to make the ultimate sacrifice for them affect them today?

Give everyone some time to write their letter. Make sure they know that their letter is between them and God and that, once they've written it, they can seal it and no one else will see it.

WATCHING OUT FOR STARS

YOU WILL NEED:

a way of making a starry ceiling (see below), a dark room, cushions and blankets to make it comfortable to lie down and stare upwards

You will need to be somewhere dark for this activity!

You will also need to think creatively about how you want to create the illusion of twinkling stars on the ceiling. Here are some ways you can do this:

- Use a projector, if you have access to one. Project an image of stars onto the ceiling using a copyright-free image found online.
- Cut out star shapes in paper and stick them over torches. Hand out torches to shine onto the ceiling.
- Use fairy lights. Even better, use star-shaped fairy lights!
- Buy a star projector. These are relatively inexpensive to buy online, but probably only worth it if you can use it for other activities too!
- Use glow-in-the-dark star stickers.

So, using your star illusion of choice, create a space that is dark and allows stars to be seen on the ceiling. Ideally, there will be space for the group to spread out and lie back to look at the 'stars'. You can make this more comfortable by putting blankets and cushions around.

Ask everyone to find a spot where it's comfortable to look up.

Once everyone is in place, explain to them (in the dark):
The star is a symbol that we use at Christmas because a star led the magi (wise men) to find Jesus. We often see an oversized star hanging above a stable in a nativity scene because of

this! The star must have been a very significant one to take these men out of their home and cause them to travel somewhere in search of a king. They knew there was something particularly special about this king for there to be a star announcing his arrival! They travelled all the way to see this king, because he meant so much to them. Maybe Jesus was a sign of hope to them, or a sign of something awesome happening on earth. Of course, Jesus meant both – new hope for everyone and there really was something truly awesome happening on earth!

Invite everyone to take some time looking up at the stars and encourage them to think about the magi searching for Jesus as they followed the star. Ask them to think about the hope that they put in the king they did not yet know. Invite them to spend some time praying in silence about the hope that they might put in Jesus today.

You could finish this time by using the words of this short and simple prayer (or inviting everyone to pray it together):

Jesus, may we be like the magi who put their hope in you and sought you out. May we notice you, remember the hope you give us and always be travelling forward to find you. Amen.

PRAYER BAUBLES

YOU WILL NEED:

air-drying clay, rolling pins, letter stamps, cookie cutters, decorative beads, a sharp pencil, ribbon, a workable surface and a wipe-clean tablecloth (if necessary)

Explain that you are going to make some baubles together to help everyone pray over Christmas, focusing on a particular word. You could suggest different words that might be good to pray about over Christmas, for example: love, gift, light, hope, comfort, joy.

Give everyone a piece of air-drying clay and invite them to roll it out, and cut out a bauble shape using cookie cutters.

Then invite them to stamp their chosen word, using letter stamps (alternatively, you could use tools or sharpened pencils), and decorate their baubles using beads pushed into the clay. Show everyone how to use a sharpened pencil to make a hole in the top of the bauble. When the clay is dry (this usually takes around 24 hours) you can put a ribbon through the hole to hang it up.

Explain that sometimes it is helpful to choose a word to focus on when you pray. Ask everyone to think about their chosen word now and pray quietly by focusing on it. Guide them through a quiet prayer: Sit comfortably. Close your eyes. Focus on breathing slowly. Then recall the word, and all the surrounding thoughts and what that word means to you. Quietly focus on that word as you breathe in and out. Talk to God as you do this.

Encourage them to pray for a short while (not too long, so that it doesn't feel unachievable or too difficult to pray like this).

CHRISTMAS CAROL PRAYERS

YOU WILL NEED:

printed copies of Christmas carols, scissors, paper, glue

This is a quirky way of writing Christmas prayers based on traditional carols. It will be a bit of fun, and hopefully a way of exploring the lyrics in carols while finding new meaning in them.

Print copies of the words from different Christmas carols. Print a few copies of each carol so that the same lines can be used twice. Carol lyrics should be available in church song books, or will be easy to find online by searching for them. Here are some examples of carols, but use your own ideas too!

Angels from the Realms of Glory
O Holy Night
Silent Night
Away in a Manger
Hark the Herald Angels Sing
In the Bleak Midwinter
The First Noel
Joy to the World
While Shepherds Watched
O Little Town of Bethlehem

Invite your group to cut up your printed carol sheets into single line pieces.

Then ask the group to take the different carol lines, mix them up and create prayers by combining them. (They can add connecting words to make the prayers make sense!)

Invite them to glue their prayers onto paper (adding the connecting words in the margins). You could play Christmas carols while they are doing this, or use this time to explore what the carols mean. Often carols have lyrics and words that seem strange or dated, and so this might be fun, or provide clarity. Depending on the group size, you could suggest that they do this in pairs.

After everyone has finished their carol prayers, end by praying these together. Take it in turns to ask each person to pray their prayer out loud.

Two fun and engaging talks to use on or around Christmas Day at an all-age service or a school or community event celebrating Christmas.

ALL-AGE TALKS

CHRISTMAS BOXES

YOU WILL NEED:

three boxes: box 1 containing lots of toy money (or you could even use the real thing!); box 2 containing a photo of a soldier; box 3 containing pictures of two or three world leaders
a basket or baby bag containing baby things – eg a baby's bottle, a nappy, a baby toy
small rewards such as sweets or stickers

Make sure that any images you use are clear enough when enlarged for everyone to see them.

Keep each item hidden until you mention it in the talk, and then invite a child to come and hold it up. Before they return to their seat you might like to give them a small reward.

TALK

Many people are very happy on Christmas Day, but many others are not. The world is in a sorry state. The reason is something the Bible calls sin – those things we all do, say and think that hurt other people and God.

When we do things that hurt God and ignore what he wants, that's sin. Sin spoils everything and gets in the way of our friendship with God.

But God is on the case – he has an amazing rescue plan for everyone, everywhere! The Bible tells us that he promises to sort out sin and all the problems it causes. So what was it that God promised to do?

Take out box 1 and invite your volunteer to open it and hold up the contents.

Did God promise to send loads and loads of **money**? Would that sort out the problems of the world caused by sin?

Take out box 2 and invite your volunteer to open it and hold up the contents.

Did God promise to send a large **army**? Would that sort out the problems of the world caused by sin?

Take out box 3 and invite your volunteer to open it and hold up the contents.

Did God promise to set up **high-level discussions** with world leaders? Would that sort out the problems of the world caused by sin?

God didn't promise any of those things! God had a much better idea – he sent us a very special gift.

Take out your baby bag or box and invite your volunteer to open it and hold up the contents.

He sent a **baby**. A baby? Why on earth did he send a baby?

How could a tiny, vulnerable baby be any good at sorting out the problems of the world?

Because, this baby was different. This baby was God himself in human form. This baby was Jesus!

Jesus came to earth as a baby on the very first Christmas Day so that one day, when he was grown up, he would put things right and sort out the sin in the world. He would make a way for everyone to be friends with God again.

That's why Jesus died on the cross. He was taking away the sins of the whole world (and that includes all the things that we have done that hurt God, too).

There is a verse in the Bible that tells us more about it. Let's listen to it now:
'… God showed how much he loved us by having Christ die for us, even though we were sinful.' Romans 5:8

So what can we do? If we are really sorry we can tell God, and he will always forgive us and give us a brand new start. Then God will help us to live his way – which is the very best way – and we can be his friends for ever and ever. What an amazing Christmas gift from God that is!

And that's what Christmas is really all about – the start of God's rescue plan for the world!

CHRISTMAS LETTERS

YOU WILL NEED:
a flip chart or a large sheet of
paper and a thick felt pen. You
may like to use the poem on
page 92 after the talk.

TALK

The following bullet points give you an outline for an all-age talk to use at your Christmas service. You can simply ad lib around the points provided or, if you prefer, write yourself a script based on these points beforehand.

- Start by finding out who was woken up the earliest, and then ask the children to tell you about one present they have received. Tell everyone about something you were given.

- Talk about the excitement of Christmas, before the actual day arrives and then on the day itself. For example: Who had an Advent calendar? Who went carol singing? Who baked their own Christmas cake? Did anyone have a turn at stirring a Christmas pudding?

- Write the letters 'C-H-R-I-S-T-M-A-S' down the side of a large sheet of paper, and invite people to suggest things about Christmas that begin with the different letters. You may get some words that relate to the real meaning of Christmas, as people will think that's what you are expecting, but write down all the suggestions! An example is given on page 92.

- Talk about the various suggestions, but then ask what is left if we take away the first six letters of the word 'Christmas'. If you are in the UK, the answer can be M&S (Marks & Spencer), but otherwise explain that we are not left with much.

- Explain that it's great to celebrate at Christmas time, and there's nothing wrong with that, but we need to remember what it is we are celebrating and that Christmas is about Christ.

- Read 2 Corinthians 9:15 to everyone: 'Thank God for his gift that is too wonderful for words!' Then, say that God sent Jesus to earth at Christmas as a very special gift – for us!

- Did anyone come up with the word 'Saviour' for the letter 'S' on the acrostic? When the angels visited the shepherds with the amazing news of Jesus' birth, they told them, 'This very day … a Saviour was born for you. He is Christ the Lord' (Luke 2:11).

- Explain that Jesus was born to save us. What from? From the very things that separate us from God – all those things we do, think and say that are wrong and not what God wants. They need to be taken away and, by dying on the cross instead of us, Jesus did just that. He took the punishment for our sins, so that all we need to do is ask God to forgive us.

- Say that in Acts 3:19 the Bible says: 'So turn to God! Give up your sins, and you will be forgiven.' Because of what Jesus has already done for us, God is waiting for us to turn to him so that he can forgive us – for ever! That's why Jesus is a very special gift to us, from God, at Christmas time.

- Invite anyone who would like to know more to come and ask one of the church leaders at the end of the service.

Walk through the Christmas story in someone else's shoes. Use these monologues to explore these familiar passages from the perspective of a shepherd, Zachariah and a wise man.

MONOLOGUES

COUNTING SHEEP

Bible reference:
Luke 2:8–16

Themes: shepherds, sheep, waiting, listening, confusion, faith, joy

Presentation style:
As a person 'in character' (include tea-towel headdress and shepherds' staff), walking around your venue.

This monologue is written from the perspective of one of the shepherds who was watching his sheep outside Bethlehem on the night that Jesus was born.

It's cold tonight. Colder than usual, I mean. I should've brought my extra blanket, or I suppose I could just snuggle down with the sheep – they're kind of like blankets, aren't they?

(He laughs awkwardly.)

Anyway, where was I? Oh, I've lost count now. I suppose I should start again.

OK – everyone, please stand still. Yes Shauna – including you. Right – Sheryl, one, Sandie, two, Sar…

Oh Sheryl – you've moved!

You know, being a shepherd can be very hard work, stuck up here out of the city, away from everyone, sometimes it's pretty lonely. And these sheep *(gestures around at imaginary sheep)*, well they're my life. If anything happened to them, even if I lost just one, it'd be the end of my world.

You know, I sometimes wonder if anyone remembers we're up here – especially at night. They're all wrapped up warm in their cosy beds, and here we are wandering the hills, keeping the wolves away.

Anyway, where was I? Oh yes, counting sheep.

Right – Sheryl, one, Sandie, two, Sarah, three, Sharlotte, four, Shau…

Oi you! Other shepherd guy!

(Waves at imaginary shepherd in the distance.)

Stop shining lights in my eyes! Stop it!

Woah!

(Falls on floor and covers eyes from imagined very bright light above.)

What is that? Is this some kind of joke? I can't see a thing. Get that light out of my face! I'm trying to count my sheep.

(Opens eyes and squints.)

It's getting brighter – can you see it? What is that? Oh my… It's got a face – and are they wings??

(Takes a moment to listen to imaginary angel.)

What do you mean I shouldn't be afraid? You're terrifying. What's that – you've got a message for me – well go on then, tell me, I'm listening…

Right, yes, OK *(nods and stares into space, as if having a conversation with an invisible angel)*, in a feeding box? Are you sure? If he's important, why is he in a feeding box? With the animals? Won't they smell? Well yes, I know I'm used to the smell of sheep. OK, OK so you want me to find one of those, in a feeding box, where the straw normally is, right. And you want me to find him now? Yes, OK, I see, if you say so.

Oh wow! There's more of you and you can sing! You're pretty good, too…

(Joins in with the angels singing – to the tune of 'O Little Town of Bethlehem'.)

'Glory to God in highest heaven, and peace to those on earth' *(continues whistling or humming tune).*

Sorry girls *(to sheep)*, but I'm off. I've got to go down into Bethlehem and find a baby, lying in a feeding box. I know, I know, it sounds crazy doesn't it, but he's not just any old baby, he's the Messiah! He's the one that's come to save us, he's the one that's going to make everything right again.

God just sent an angel, well a whole group of angels, actually, to tell me about this super special baby. I know! It's amazing isn't it?! But why me? Well I don't know, I mean I'm just a scruffy little shepherd, but he must've wanted to tell me, otherwise he wouldn't have sent an angel would he?!

No *(talking to sheep again)*, I don't know when I'll be back, you'll just have to be good, won't you? Shauna – you're in charge – no that doesn't mean you get all the straw – it means you're in charge of sharing out the straw! Just do what I'd do, OK!

(Shepherd departs whistling or humming 'O Little Town of Bethlehem' and skipping as he goes.)

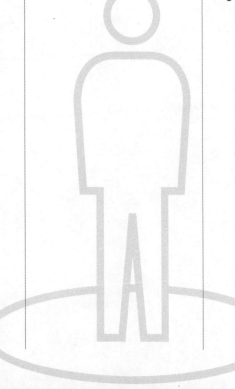

DUMBSTRUCK!

Bible reference:
Luke 1:8–24

Themes: angels, obedience, trust, faith, hope, prophecy, Holy Spirit, gifts, joy, calling, commitment

Presentation style: Clearly, since Zechariah is unable to speak, this is an internal monologue that is externally audible to the congregation. It will be most effective delivered from the front of your meeting space with Zechariah simply sat on a chair. If possible, prerecord the monologue and play it as Zechariah simply sits on his chair.

This monologue is written from the perspective of Zechariah after he has been made unable to speak in the Temple, following his questioning of the angel who came to tell Zechariah of John's future birth.

Oh no! Oh no! I'm thinking words, I'm moving my mouth like I normally do, but nothing is coming out! No one can hear me, they think I've gone mad! They keep telling me I'm not saying anything, and I keep trying to explain that I am saying things, but I can only hear them in my head, and they're not coming out of my mouth as noises!

How could he do this to me? Well, I suppose it was my own fault, really, I should just have believed what he said. He was an angel, after all. And now I've got nine months of this – not being able to speak. Great.

I suppose you might be wondering how all this happened – seeing an angel isn't exactly a usual occurrence, even for people serving in the Temple!

So, there always has to be one of us in the Temple, burning incense, praying and making sure everyone else can pray at the Temple, too. It's just part of what we do – and well, this morning it was my turn.

I was doing my job, it was all going well and then right there in front of me an angel appeared. I very nearly fell over backwards and I was so scared I thought I might faint! The angel was trying to be friendly, and he told me not to be afraid, but I mean he was pretty scary – he kind of glowed and everything.

And then he said something I really wasn't expecting.

Before I tell you what he said, let's just get one thing straight – I'm pretty old, and so is my wife Elizabeth. And old people don't tend to suddenly have babies. That's just not how things work, is it?

Anyway, back to what the angel said.

'Your wife is going to have a baby boy and you have to call him John,' said the angel. And then he said all sorts of other wonderful things about what John would do, like bringing people back to God and being filled with the Holy Spirit and more awesome stuff.

But I just didn't know what to say. To be honest, I couldn't really get past the whole 'your wife is going to have a baby' thing – we're not exactly in the right time of life, like I said!

On reflection, it probably wasn't the best idea to ask the angel what he was on about. I mean, I just wanted to know how it was going to work – we're too old to have babies in any normal kind of way.

But then, when he said his name was Gabriel and God had sent him personally to tell me about my part in his awesome plan, I realised I should've trusted God to sort it out all along. But it was too late, because then Gabriel said because I didn't believe what he'd said the first time round, I'd not be able to speak until John was born.

I was so excited about what had happened that I knew I had to get outside and tell everyone straight away – only when I got out there I remembered that I couldn't speak. I tried to tell them with sign language, but they couldn't make out what I was saying at all. The closest they got was that a large bird was in the Temple and that I was going to lay an egg. In the end I gave up trying and came home.

And then, of course, I had to try and tell Elizabeth about the whole thing without using any words – that was interesting – but we got there in the end – and I think, well, I hope she knows what's going to happen!

NOT SO WISE?

Bible reference:
Matthew 2:1–12

Themes: trust, faith, obedience, gifts, following, Messiah, commitment

Presentation style: Either as a reflective reading or as a person 'in character' on 'stage'.

This monologue is written from the perspective of a fourth wise man, who is sceptical of his three friends and their belief that a new star in the sky signifies the birth of a new and very important King.

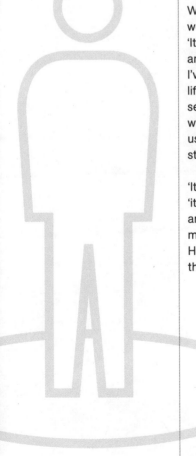

I don't know, I just don't know. The things people do, eh? I'm sure they seem totally sane when you're on the inside, but when you're on the outside – well, let me tell you, they look pretty bizarre!

I don't know what got into them, really. We were just outside, a while back now, looking at the stars just as we normally do, and then those three, well they couldn't contain themselves! They kept jumping up and down and pointing at this particularly bright star.

When I asked them why they were so excited they just said, 'It's the star! Look at it! It's amazing! It's so bright!' I mean, I've seen plenty of stars in my lifetime, in fact I've probably seen more than most, but they were convinced that none of us had ever seen this star before.

'It's new!' they kept on saying, 'it's new, it means something amazing has happened! It means a new king will be born! He's going to be the King of the Jews!'

'Well, it could mean that,' I said, 'if it is actually new. I mean, we might just have not noticed it before.' But they were adamant, this was a brand new star that had a very specific meaning.

And then, as if that wasn't crazy enough, they decided they'd go and tell King Herod that they'd seen a new star, which meant there was a new king. I mean, I don't know about you, but I'd be pretty cross if I was the king of somewhere, and some random men came and told me there was another king instead of me! That doesn't strike me as a particularly wise thing to tell a king like Herod. But, anyway, they seemed to think it would be a good idea – and that Herod would tell them where they could find this new baby 'King of the Jews'.

So they just went. They left me here all on my own – and that was weeks ago! And they took a bunch of strange things with them, too.

Gold, frankincense and myrrh. I mean, taking gold for a new king, that's kind of obvious, right? He's special, he's a king, of course he'll need gold. And frankincense, well it does smell pretty good, and if you're a king then you don't want to smell bad, but myrrh – why would you take that to a newborn king? They put myrrh on dead bodies – why would a new and very alive little baby need that?

I hope they're OK, actually, I mean I might think they're crazy, but I don't want Herod to do anything nasty to them, he's not exactly known for being Mr Nice Guy! Do you think maybe I should go to Jerusalem and check on them? But then if I went, who would stay here and keep looking at all these stars?

I suppose it is a particularly bright one isn't it? And I'm sure we would've noticed a star that bright if it had been there before. Maybe it is new. Oh, but if it is then I've totally messed up, haven't I? I should've gone with them in the first place – I want to see this new King too. He sounds amazing. A king of the Jews – he could be the Messiah! In fact, there's no one else he could be! Oh it's all starting to make sense now. Woah!

O CHRISTMAS TREE,
O CHRISTMAS TREE...

Bible reference:
Isaiah 9:6,7

Themes: good news, Christian traditions, mission, nativity, church, consumerism, integrity, authenticity

Presentation style: Dressed as a Christmas tree that is decorated with the items mentioned, or delivered as a voice-over with a static and accordingly decorated Christmas tree at the front of your venue.

This monologue is written from the perspective of a contemporary Christmas tree, in a Christian home on Christmas Day morning.

I love Christmas. It's when I get to come inside, into the warm. I get extra water and lovely accessories, and I feel super glamorous. I even get to look after everyone's presents under my branches. Everyone smiles whenever they see me, and whenever there are visitors, they always comment on my beauty…

I'm sorry, where are my manners, let me introduce myself. My name is Norman, I'm a Nordmann Fir Tree, I'm 7 years old and I've been helping the Smith family celebrate Christmas since I was just a wee toddler.

Only this year, things seem a little bit different and I'm not quite sure why. Usually, I've had lots of smelly pine cones, mini santa hats, dangly icicles, tinkly bells and big round shiny things stuck all over me. Oh, and then they put this itchy silver stuff on top, too. But this year I've got some new accessories! And guess what? They're mini-people!

In fact there's even one mini-person that looks a bit like he's in a cardboard box filled with straw! And then there are three old men with long beards and they're carrying little presents, and then there's a flock of sheep and two little people with bendy sticks that look like they might be shepherds, and then there's a woman in a blue dress and a man in what looks a bit like a stripy bath robe. Oh, and a cow or two as well.

I suppose the biggest change is that, on my big spiky top branch, instead of a giant purple santa hat (*it has sparkles and plays 'When Santa got stuck up the chimney' when you squeeze the pom pom!*), this year there's an enormous glowing star! It flashes and everything!

Maybe they just thought it was time for a few new bits and pieces, right? I mean some of my other accessories were getting a bit tired, I guess. But then that wouldn't explain why they've got some more mini-people in a little mini-hut over there by the fire – in fact, they're kind of similar to these ones here on my branches.

And last night, I heard everyone talking about going somewhere this morning. And I guess they must've gone, because, well, the house seems pretty empty to me today. I'm used to the kids running down the stairs as soon as the sun comes up, poking and shaking all the presents I'm looking after, but this morning they're not here.

I think they said they were going to 'birch'. Or something like that. I know there's a birch tree out in the garden, opposite my usual spot, but I can't see why they'd have gone out to say 'Hi' to him – I mean all his leaves have fallen off at this time of year, he just looks like a big bald twig.

Well, whatever it is they're doing, it must be something pretty important to be putting off getting stuck into all these exciting parcels and, of course, telling me how lovely I look. I mean, today is my day isn't it?! Christmas Day – it's all about me! What am I supposed to do with my lovely Smithses?

(*Sounds tearful and begins to sniffle a little.*)

I suppose I'll just have to sing to myself to keep me company.

(*Begins to sing 'O Christmas Tree, O Christmas Tree'.*)

Oh hey! I think they're back. I can hear the key in the door. Yay they're home, present time, present time, present time!

Everyone is so excited, I'm so glad they're back. They must be excited about all their presents, I'm sure. But hold on a minute, what are they talking about? Cheese? Oh right, of course, they like to eat that after their enormous feast.

Cheese-us? Well I suppose that's one way of saying you're looking forward to cheese, no that's not quite it, Jee-sus.

What is that?

(*Pauses, as if listening to something.*)

No way! Wow! I can't believe it! It all makes so much sense now! I've just heard some incredible news, and it just totally blew my mind. Well, it ruffled my pine needles anyhow!

Christmas isn't all about presents, it's not even all about me, it's all about this tiny little baby, the one in the cardboard box with the straw in it! He's not just any old baby – he's God! The God! The one who made everything, even me!

God came down to earth as a tiny baby because he loves everyone so, so much. He wanted us all to see just how much we mean to him, and that's why he came. This baby went on to do some absolutely incredible things when he grew up, and in the end he did something so, so, so, so, so incredible to show how much he loves us. And Christmas? Well that's all about celebrating the start of this story, when God gave us the best present ever! Wow!

So that's what Christmas is all about! I'm just here to help make the celebration all the more fun. Cool! I'm pretty proud of these mini people on my branches now – they remind me what I'm really here for.

Is it present time?

Explore the Christmas story as a community of all ages.

ALL-AGE SERVICES

GROWING TOGETHER IN GOD

YOU WILL NEED:
- different-sized circles made from different coloured card, for the congregation to choose one as they enter church (alternatively, you could use milk carton lids)
- a tree trunk made from brown card
- brown chunky wool or ribbon, several lengths
- a large gold star, based on a cross shape
- a thank-you card or banner
- a trowel
- a watering can
- plant food
- large jigsaw pieces
- 9 bauble-shaped pieces of card with the words 'love, joy, peace, patience, kindness, goodness, faithfulness, gentleness, self-control' on them
- blank bauble and star-shaped pieces of card for prayers
- pencils and pens
- hyacinth bulbs (optional)

Welcome your congregation and explain that today you'll be thinking about growing together in God, using the image of a Christmas tree to help you.

Sing together as you begin your service.

INTRODUCTION

We are all God's people. We are all similar, and yet all different, each of us coming with our own gifts and talents, problems and pains.

We make up God's church and we are meant to work together to share the good news of Jesus.

You should have been given a card circle as you arrived (*check that everyone has a circle, and distribute any extras required*). Look at one side of your circle. Hold it in your hand and think of something that you are good at – a talent or gift that God has given you. Turn the circle over. Now think of something that you find difficult – a situation or problem that you are facing at the moment.

Invite your congregation to pray together using the following words:

Lord, thank you for all the different people here that make up your church – each one so gifted and talented, each one also with so many things on their mind that they struggle with. Help us to trust you with our talents and our troubles. Amen

Ask each person to bring forward their circle to create a triangle-shaped tree on the floor at the front of your meeting space, starting with one circle at the top. You might like to play some quiet background music while people come forward.

Sing together as an alternative – invite everyone to join in with a congregational time of worship, using a song that people are likely to be familiar with so that they are able to join in as they come up to the front.

When everyone who wants to has added their circle to the tree and returned to their seats, continue with the following words:

We all know that trees are made up of several parts – the trunk, branches, roots, leaves and sometimes fruit. Let's take a moment to consider how the different parts of the Christmas tree can help us to think about how we grow as Christians.

Add the trunk to the circle tree.

In John 15:5 Jesus said: 'I am the vine, and you are the branches.' That's a bit like saying he is the trunk of the tree and we are the branches. The trunk of a tree is strong. It is at the centre, at the heart of the tree. It carries all the nutrients to the branches.

Only when the branches are attached to the trunk of the tree can they receive nutrients and water. That's what they need to help them grow leaves and fruit. We all know that when a branch is broken off from a tree, it quickly withers and dies.

I wonder if each one of us has Jesus at the centre of our lives, so that we can grow as Christians and bear good fruit in our lives.

Allow time for everyone to consider their response to this question, and then move into a time of sung worship.

Sing together a suitable song.

After your time of sung worship, continue with these words:

Have you ever looked at tree roots? They're amazing. They create a network of thick and thin hairs that anchor the tree down into the soil. They strengthen the tree and keep it strong when the wind blows. They provide nutrients for the tree that help it to grow. If the roots aren't healthy, the tree will soon die.

At this point you might like to invite any children in the congregation to come forward and use wool and ribbon to create some roots for your circle tree.

In the Bible, in Colossians 2:7, Paul encourages Christians to keep their lives rooted in Jesus, and by doing so to stay strong in their faith.

Are the roots in your walk with Jesus healthy? They won't just stay healthy by themselves, it takes effort to keep ourselves rooted in Christ. There are a few things we can do, though, that will help us to maintain our roots.

As you talk about maintaining good roots, you may choose to place the items mentioned around the roots of your circle tree.

First, we should try to be rooted in gratefulness – saying 'thank you' for all the good things we have in our lives *(thank-you card or banner)*. Secondly, we can make an effort to cultivate the soil of our lives by weeding out unhelpful habits or ways of thinking *(trowel)*. Thirdly, we need to feed our roots and keep them healthy by spending time talking with and listening to God and reading his word *(watering can and plant food)*. Finally, we can help our roots stay strong by staying connected to others in God's family *(jigsaw pieces)*.

Explain that you're now going to think about the leaves on a tree and the fruit that it might bear.

Most trees have leaves, and some have fruit at certain times of year. Even evergreen trees, such as fir trees, only grow fir cones at a certain time of year. Our lives can be a bit seasonal, too. We won't always be ready to bear fruit, and sometimes we'll go through a season that feels a lot like winter – in which we need to take time out to rest and be restored. But, when the time is right, God will help us to bear good fruit for him, as he fills us with his Holy Spirit.

In Galatians 5:22 Paul describes the fruit of the Spirit as: love, joy, peace, patience, kindness, goodness, faithfulness, gentleness, self-control. These are the fruits that God wants to nurture in our lives.

As you name each fruit, add the relevant card bauble to the tree.

Which fruit of the Spirit could you ask God to help you with this Christmas?

Allow time for everyone to consider their response to this question.

Sing together a suitable song.

Continue with these words:

There are still a few things missing from our Christmas tree. First, a star. Today, I'm going to use a specially-shaped star for the top of our tree, one that has the cross at the centre of it. Because the cross is at the centre of the Christmas story – it's the very reason that Jesus came to earth. It's only through Jesus dying on the cross and being raised to life that we can be friends with God. That's what our star will represent today – Jesus and all he has done for us!

As you say this, place the star at the top of the tree.

You might also have noticed that our tree has no decorations and that's where you come in!

Encourage people to come forward and collect a star- or bauble-shaped piece of card. Invite them to write the name of someone they would like to pray for, then add their decoration to the tree.

Sing a final song together and, as they do so, encourage people to pray for everyone named on the tree.

As people leave, you might like to give a hyacinth bulb to each child to plant at home as a reminder of all they have learnt today about growing closer to God.

ALL-AGE SERVICES

02

THE WONDER OF CHRISTMAS

This service will help your congregation to engage with the traditional nativity story in a new way. You will need to allow time for a little preparation before the service to ensure that everything runs smoothly.

YOU WILL NEED:
- 6 star parts as outlined below
- 5 large star shapes cut from card
- star-shaped gift tags (enough for each member of the congregation to have one)

Before the service:
Prepare six large star parts with pictures of Bible characters as shown in the diagram on page 93. (If you do not wish to literally create these, you could always create a similar visual effect using PowerPoint.)

Star part 1 – Mary
Star part 2 – Joseph
Star part 3 – angels
Star part 4 – wise men
Star part 5 – you
Central heart piece

Prepare five large stars for prayers. On one side of all the stars write the word 'Wonderful'. On the other side draw or attach an image of: a seed growing, an elephant, Mary and baby Jesus, an empty cross, the word 'Wow' – one image or word per star.

Welcome your congregation, and explain that today's theme will be awe and wonder.

Sing together as you begin your service.

INTRODUCTION

Invite everyone to be quiet for a moment, taking some time to reflect. After a few minutes' silence, slowly read out the following:

Wonder is the beginning of wisdom, wonder is the start of worship, wonder is spontaneous praise. I wonder what makes you wonder? What is it that gives you joy; amazes you, delights you, makes you say 'WOW!'?

Something large – maybe a sunset, a mountain, a roaring waterfall?
Or something small – a child's hand in yours, a seed, bread?

Picture one thing in your mind that fills you with wonder and now give thanks to God for it.

Choose an appropriate way for your congregation to give thanks. This might be in a short quiet time of personal prayer with background music, an interactive activity such as blowing bubbles to help focus thoughts, or you might choose to create a PowerPoint presentation of images that inspire wonder.

Children are so much better at wonder than adults. They peer intently at piles of soil, they examine every detail of a daisy in the grass, they freely play with almost anything that nature provides. For children, everything is amazing, everything is exciting, new, fresh and wonderful. Perhaps we need to reclaim our childhood wonder and allow it to develop our faith.

Sing a song of praise – encouraging the younger members to help the older members to worship with wonder. Before singing this song, you might invite people to shout out things that fill them with wonder. Or depending upon which song you choose, there might be an appropriate time to do this between verses.

After your time of sung worship, say the following prayer together:

Wow! Father God, you are a wonderful creator. We give you thanks for all that you have given us. Help us to be like children as we appreciate the wonder of your world. Amen

CHRISTMAS STORY WONDER

Invite everyone to sit down, and explain that you're going to look at the Christmas story in five parts, using a star shape to help you. You can use the script below, or edit it to better suit your congregation.

We have so much, see so much, know so much, and are connected so well globally – yet how often do we allow ourselves to be truly amazed? How often do we live enough in the present (rather than the past or the future) to look beyond ourselves, to say: 'WOW! That is absolutely amazing!'?

We so often take everyday things for granted: the intricacy of a flower, the complexity of the human body, the detail in our fingerprints, the cycle of day and night, the cry of a newborn baby… Let's allow ourselves to be still and wonder now, as we consider again the Christmas story.

Using a child-friendly Bible, read the Christmas story out to your congregation. Alternatively, you might choose to act out the story with a few volunteers, or perhaps watch a suitable video clip.

Explain that you are going to show some images representing parts of the Christmas story, and invite everyone to wonder together about the part of the story that is represented.

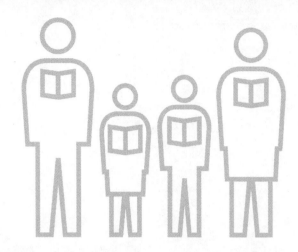

Show star part 1.

Wonder at Mary's simple willingness to say to God, 'your will be done'. Don't forget that Mary was a young girl, probably only 14 or 15 years old. She wasn't married and she was pregnant – that made everything pretty complicated! Can you say yes to God?

Show star part 2.

Wonder at Joseph's faithfulness in God to keep his promises. Joseph trusted that God would do just as he said he would. Do you keep your promises? Are you faithful to God?

Show star part 3.

Wonder at angels visiting the shepherds. Wonder at the willingness of the shepherds to leave their sheep and visit their Saviour. Are there things you would be willing to leave behind to draw closer to God?

Show star part 4.

Wonder at the wise men who studied the stars and understood the meaning of a new star in the sky. How has your studying of the Bible helped you in meeting with Jesus?

Show star part 5.

Wonder at your own response to all that you know of the Christmas story. How do you feel about all this? Is there a character you identify with most?

Sing an appropriate song of worship together, encouraging your congregation to continue their wondering as they sing.

THE HEART OF CHRISTMAS
Draw everyone's attention to the fact that your star seems to have a hole in the middle – clearly there is something missing! As you place the central heart piece into the star, use the following words:

There's something wonderful at the centre of our Christmas star that's missing…

Add heart piece.

Of course, it's Jesus, but wait, let's remember how wonderful he is…

This is our God. The God who created the universe, set the stars into space, created the earth and all living things. He is the one who made us and who chose to come down to earth as a baby and be born into a dirty stable, wrapped in strips of cloth – and for what? For us – for you, for me – out of love for each one of us.
Wow! And if that isn't enough wonder for you, then I don't know what is!

PRAYERS
Explain to your congregation that you will now spend some time in prayer together. Collect your five large stars and invite children or families to come forward and hold them up for you. Everyone should begin by holding their star with the 'Wonderful' side facing the congregation. As you pray together, turn the stars over one by one.

Invite your congregation to join in by using the response **Wow! Thank you, wonderful God** at the end of each prayer:

Wow! Lord, you made the smallest atom and the tiniest seed, things that we cannot even see with our eyes, and yet they all go together to make up our wonderful world. Thank you, Lord.
Wow! Thank you, wonderful God

Wow! Lord, you made the largest things – elephants, whales, our planet earth, galaxies, the universe and all that is in it. Thank you, Lord.
Wow! Thank you, wonderful God

Wow! Lord, you sent your Son, Jesus, as a tiny baby born to Mary, and gave us the gift of the wonderful Christmas story. Thank you, Lord.
Wow! Thank you, wonderful God

Wow! Lord, you lived an amazing life on earth, teaching, healing the sick, raising the dead, dying on the cross and being raised to life again so that all people could be your friend. Thank you, Lord.
Wow! Thank you, wonderful God

Wow! Lord, thank you for the gift of awe and wonder. Thank you that we can learn so much from the lives of children about this gift. May we use it to increase our faith and share your love with others.
Wow! Thank you, wonderful God

If you have a Christmas tree in your church, you could add these large prayer stars to it as decorations.

Sing together a final song of worship as you celebrate all that God has done.

AFTERWARDS
Give out silver and gold star-shaped gift tags for people to take away and encourage them to write their own 'Wonder-full' prayers on them and place them on their Christmas tree at home.

HOW TO...
EXPLORE TOGETHER

Within our faith communities there is a rich diversity of God's people all at different stages in their faith development and spiritual experience, and all with different learning needs and preferences. We are a beautiful collection of artists, scholars, reflectors, dancers, data collectors, fact finders, readers, sculptors, writers, musicians, actors, talkers and listeners.

Explore Together places the Bible at the centre of this diversity. It is a new and practical tool for helping people to explore God's Word and hear his voice in a way that embraces their natural preferences. At the heart of Explore Together is a desire to see people hear from God and learn more of his love for them. It works with big groups, small groups, mixed-age groups, single-age groups, older people, young people, children, families, house groups, church congregations, youth groups, school groups… in fact, Explore Together can be used in any environment with any group dynamic.

THE SIX STEPS

There are six essential steps to an Explore Together session, each of which can be tailored to slot into any existing structure and space:

1 Preparation
2 Presenting the Bible
3 Prayer
4 Exploring
5 Sharing
6 Giving thanks

Step four provides an opportunity for people to engage with God's Word using the Explore Together questions and the six Explore Together zones. Each zone has been carefully designed to cater for particular learning needs and preferences:

 Colour Zone
for those who learn by seeing

 Listening Zone
for those who learn by hearing

 Chat Zone
for those who learn by thinking aloud

 Word Zone
for those who learn by reading

 Busy Zone
for those who learn by doing

 Quiet Zone
for those who learn by reflecting

Individuals can choose to spend all of their exploring time in one zone, but may also choose to visit several zones, depending upon their preferences. There is no right or wrong amount of time to spend in a zone.

It is quite deliberate that no specific instructions are provided for each zone. Individuals are free to engage however they like with the resources provided in each area as they consider the Explore Together questions for the session.

If you'd like to know more about the ideas that underpin Explore Together and hear about our experiences of Explore Together in action please read our companion book:

Explore Together: The Journey

FREQUENTLY ASKED QUESTIONS

Our church has many people/a few people. Will Explore Together work here?

Over the last five years we have seen Explore Together used in small groups with only a few individuals but also in larger settings. We have known Explore Together to be used within a family home, but also within a programme at Spring Harvest for 450 children.

Key to the smooth running of Explore Together is preparation and planning. It is important to consider how the participants will arrange themselves into small groups. There is a danger that individuals who are close friends, or of similar age and background, will organise themselves into groups, therefore missing out on the excellent opportunity to learn from those who are at a different age or stage in their lives. Inclusivity is key if individuals want to be challenged to learn something new.

While the planning, organisation and setting up of the zones are essential, large or small numbers of people do not present a challenge. No matter how large the group is, Step 5: Sharing is always done in small groups of three to five people. When feeding back in larger churches or groups, having a group of people with roving radio microphones in the congregation works very well.

Isn't Explore Together a bit chaotic, especially with children present?

It is chaotic in the sense that everyone is engaging in different ways, but not because the children are present. The explore zones are designed to embrace a range of learning preferences. Individuals of all ages very quickly find their own preferred activity and become occupied. Although there might be a buzz in the room, activity will be purposeful, colourful and appealing, and everyone has the freedom to move around and make choices in a safe and supportive environment. Many adults find the kinaesthetic dimension of Explore Together appealing too!

Does Explore Together need a lot of space? We have fixed pews in our church building that often restrict what we can do.

Explore Together can be planned carefully to fit flexibly into spaces that are different in size and organised in different ways. The explore zones do not all need to happen in one room, they could be spread out to happen in different areas. Your choice of activities can also be tailored to the amount of space you have, and you can creatively use the edges and corners of a room that contains pews. The smallest setting for Explore Together that we have heard about is at a dining room table in a family home.

What if someone says something completely off-the-wall?

My immediate response to this question is, 'it's better out than in'. What better place is there to explore your faith and ask your questions than in a community of faith – a community made up of many people with varying levels of understanding, wisdom, knowledge and experience? Explore Together provides a safe environment for people to express their thoughts and ideas, some of which may otherwise never be aired or challenged. The questions help to provide safe boundaries and keep the focus on the desirable aims and outcomes.

Simeon and Anna

Luke 2:21–38   Themes: celebration, Christmas, thanksgiving, prophesy, salvation, blessing

Forty days after Jesus had been born his parents took him to the Temple to present him to God, as was the Jewish custom. Upon arriving at the Temple, Joseph and Mary encountered Simeon and Anna who gave thanks for Jesus and spoke of his future.

Prepare

Resources required

- Simeon and Anna's monologues
- 'Simeon and Anna' audio recording (from *The Big Bible Storybook* audio book)
- 'Simeon and Anna' story text (from *The Big Bible Storybook*)
- additional prayer activity
- incarnation quotes word collection
- 'Simeon and Anna' image collection
- light image collection
- Luke 2:21–38 (CEV)
- 'Simeon and Anna' Explore Together questions (PDF and PowerPoint)

All available from www.exploretogether.org

You will also need to gather:

- a recording of the Nunc Dimittis (Simeon's song) – various versions of this song are available; choose one that best suits (or perhaps challenges!) your community
- Scratch Art doodle sheets
- a selection of used Christmas cards (both nativity and non-nativity)
- glitter
- beads and thread
- embroidery silks, aida fabric, threads and blunt needles

Presenting the Bible

With the community gathered together, begin by sharing the words from Luke 2:21–38. Consider carefully which version of the Bible you choose to read from.

Alternatively or in addition you may choose to use:
- Simeon and Anna's monologues

Without being tempted to answer them, introduce the following questions to your community for them to consider:

- **Why is this story good news for you?**
- **Why is this story good news for your neighbours?**
- **How can you be a light that draws all mankind to God?**
- **How can we as a community be a light that draws all mankind to God?**

Pray

Pray for and with your community, asking God to help you hear from him. This time of prayer can be creative, interactive, responsive, meditative or sung. It could also include communion and intercession. Ensure that there is a place set aside where people can go if they feel that they need someone to pray with them specifically. Have a small team of people available to offer prayer if required. Prayer ministry should be available throughout an Explore Together session.

Explore

Read out your questions from Step 2 again or display them on a screen. Remind your community to consider these questions as they separate into their explore zones. Some may choose to consider all the questions while others may focus on just one. Some may completely ignore the questions and just open themselves up to God.

Invite your community to separate into small groups, around the zone(s) of their preference. Explain that individuals are welcome to spend as much or as little time in each zone as they wish, engaging at whatever level they feel comfortable. Depending upon where your quiet zone is located, you may wish to provide directions and remind people not to disturb one another when using this space.

Colour Zone

- coloured pastels, crayons and various colours and sizes of paper
- 'Simeon and Anna' image collection
- light image collection
- Scratch Art doodle sheets
- used Christmas cards, glue, scissors and glitter for collage
- copies of the 'Simeon and Anna' ET questions

Listening Zone

- 'Simeon and Anna' audio recording (from *The Big Bible Storybook* audio book)
- a recording of the Nunc Dimittis
- copies of the 'Simeon and Anna' ET questions

Chat Zone

- a separate area with chairs, cushions or beanbags
- a chat zone host who is willing to read the passage again and then lead a discussion around the questions
- copies of Luke 2:21–38 (CEV) or Bibles
- copies of the 'Simeon and Anna' ET questions

Word Zone

- pens, pencils, paper
- biblical commentaries relating to Luke 2:21–38
- 'Simeon and Anna' story text
- other children's Bibles and Bible story books containing a version of Luke 2:21–38
- 'Simeon and Anna' story text (from *The Big Bible Storybook*)
- copies of Luke 2:21–38 (CEV) or Bibles
- incarnation quotes word collection
- copies of the 'Simeon and Anna' ET questions

Busy Zone

- plasticine, play dough or clay
- pipe cleaners
- beads and thread
- embroidery silks, aida fabric, threads and blunt needles
- junk modelling items
- masking tape, glue and scissors
- copies of the 'Simeon and Anna' ET questions

Quiet Zone

- a separate area where people can be alone with their thoughts and God
- 'Simeon and Anna' image collection (optional)
- light image collection (optional)
- copies of Luke 2:21–38 (CEV) or Bibles
- copies of the 'Simeon and Anna' ET questions

Share

As your time for exploring together draws to a close, invite your community to come back together into small groups of three to five. Suggest that they share their responses to the questions posed at the beginning.

Giving thanks

Invite the explorers to share their reflections with the wider community, drawing together their responses and noting any common themes that emerge. Conclude by reading Luke 2:21–38 again (from the same Bible version used earlier). Then lead your community in a prayer, thanking God for all that he has revealed through this story. Encourage your community to continue their conversations about this story as they leave, and to take with them any artwork/writings/thoughts from the session.

Christmas is a great opportunity to run events that can help your church reach out to your community. These two family fun-day outlines offer comprehensive plans for running a community event with a Christmas theme.

FAMILY FUN DAYS

FAMILY FUN DAY
IN THE LIGHT OF ADVENT

A family reflective event with different areas to explore. It will work best if someone is present in each area to facilitate and help with the activity there.

YOU WILL NEED:
- 3 large central candles (preferably slightly different sizes for effect)
- a tray of sand
- tea lights
- a taper (make sure you do a health and safety risk assessment when using candles and tapers, and always make sure you have a bucket of water handy!)
- a world map on screen
- 2 planks of wood
- 3 large nails
- a piece of fabric for each focus area (on which to place the items for that area)
- specific items for each focus area

When everyone has arrived, begin by introducing your event and then explaining the theme for your time together.

The theme for today is 'In the light of advent', so first let us remember together that 'God is light and doesn't have any darkness in him' (1 John 1:5).

Light candle one.

During his time on earth, Jesus said, 'I am the light for the world! Follow me, and you won't be walking in the dark. You will have the light that gives life' (John 8:12). Let's look together at this map of the world, and remember all of the good things that Jesus brings.

Display the map of the world on screen and pause for a few moments.

Light candle two.

The God who said, 'Let light shine out of darkness' made his light shine in our hearts. God gives us this light through Jesus. We have this light through God's Holy Spirit in us.

Set up two pieces of wood laid out as a cross, with three nails.

Light candle three.

As we look at the three candles, representing Father, Son and Holy Spirit, let's ask God to make his light strong in each of us, so that others can glimpse God and recognise him.

Invite everyone to join you in the words of the following prayer:

Lord, help us to spend time with you today so that you can fan into flame your light within our hearts. Amen

Today is space for you to spend time with God using the different focus areas to help and allow his light to work through you and in you.

Explain the layout of your focus areas, and any practical arrangements for using them.

1

FOCUS AREA 1
In the Light of Advent... Be still...

You will need: black pens, paper, cross and candle outlines, example finished cross or candle, lantern in centre with candle

Activity: drawing, using crosses and candle shapes

Instructions: Split the cross and candle outlines into sections with a black fine liner, then try a different doodle in each section. As you doodle, let the rhythm of the drawing lead you into thinking about and talking quietly with God.

2

FOCUS AREA 2
In the Light of Advent... Wait...

You will need: a calendar with the days crossed off, traffic light at amber picture, sand egg timer, stopwatch, plastic pots, plastic container of compost, flower bulbs, stickers and pens

Activity: thinking about waiting and planting bulbs

Instructions: Waiting can be very difficult. We often find ourselves anxious to be getting on with the next thing, but the Bible is full of encouragement to wait for God's timing. Hold a flower bulb carefully in your hand. Think about how long it takes to grow into a flower. Waiting can sometimes be for the best!

Take a bulb and plant it in soil, label your pot and take it home. As you care for your plant, waiting patiently for it to grow, remember that God often asks us to wait.

FOCUS AREA 3
In the Light of Advent… Prepare…

You will need: a duster, furniture polish, a dustpan and brush, clean sheets and a pillow case, a washing-up bowl, a pair of rubber gloves, washing-up liquid, tea cups and a teapot, a to do list for Christmas, wrapping paper, sticky tape, Christmas labels, scissors, tree decorations, a mini Christmas tree or branch in a pot, pens

Activity: thinking about preparing for Christmas

Instructions: Think and talk about all the things that are prepared for Christmas. Sometimes it's easy to get carried away with all the preparations – so much so that we forget the real meaning of Christmas. In the Bible, many people prepared the way for Jesus, in a way that was special to them.

John prepared the way for Jesus, Mary prepared herself to give birth to the Messiah, Joseph prepared to marry Mary, the shepherds were prepared to leave their sheep, the wise men prepared to visit Jesus and give gifts.

Advent is partly about preparing for Christmas and partly about preparing for Jesus' return to earth. Listen to what Jesus said to his friend Martha, about taking time out to be with him.

Ask a volunteer in this area to read out the following:

The Lord and his disciples were traveling along and came to a village. When they got there, a woman named Martha welcomed him into her home. She had a sister named Mary, who sat down in front of the Lord and was listening to what he said. Martha was worried about all that had to be done. Finally, she went to Jesus and said, 'Lord, doesn't it bother you that my sister has left me to do all the work by myself? Tell her to come and help me!'

The Lord answered, 'Martha, Martha! You are worried and upset about so many things, but only one thing is necessary. Mary has chosen what is best, and it will not be taken away from her.'

Luke 10:38–42

Can you think of one thing that would help you to spend time with Jesus this Advent? Maybe you could deliberately say grace together at mealtimes, or light an Advent candle together each day, or perhaps join together to bless different people in prayer or action. Talk with your group to come up with a plan, and then write or draw your idea on a gift tag and hang it on the tree.

FOCUS AREA 4
In the Light of Advent… Pray…

You will need: names of different countries on separate slips of paper in a basket, a large labyrinth drawn out on an old sheet or large piece of fabric with a globe or world map at the centre

Activity: praying for the world

Instructions: The Bible tells us, 'Don't worry about anything, but pray about everything. With thankful hearts offer up your prayers and requests to God' (Philippians 4:6).

Think of those around the world and close to home who have little or no light this Advent season, those who are struggling and overwhelmed by the darkness around them.

Choose a country from the basket. Take it with you as you slowly walk the labyrinth to the centre where you will find a map of the world. Pray for God's light to shine into the lives of people who live in the country on your slip of paper, and then leave the paper at the centre of the labyrinth. Walk slowly back to the beginning of the labyrinth trusting that God always hears your prayers.

FOCUS AREA 5
In the Light of Advent… Give…

You will need: a nativity scene, a cross, a selection of parcels, lining paper, a large ink pad, pens, wet wipes and a waste bin or bag

Activity: looking at the nativity scene and the cross

Instructions: Look at the nativity scene and think about God sending his only Son to be born on earth and to die for us. This Advent, what can you give back to him? Love, time, a listening ear, a helping hand or something else?

Press your hand into the ink pad. Make your mark on the paper, then draw or write beside the hand print what you can give to God.

FOCUS AREA 6
In the Light of Advent… Shine…

You will need: a table or desk lamp, torches, shiny stars, sun and moon images, yellow or orange fabric, glow sticks

Activity: thinking about being like light

Instructions: In the Bible, Jesus says, 'I am the light for the world! Follow me, and you won't be walking in the dark. You will have the light that gives life' (John 8:12). Jesus also said that we can be like light to the world, too, if we let our light shine. We should shine like stars in the sky (Philippians 2:15).

Think about how you might shine for Jesus and talk with your group about it, as you take a glow stick and crack it so that it shines.

In the Light of Advent…
Give Thanks & Celebrate

You will need: an Advent wreath, a calendar, a large candle, party poppers

Bring your congregation back together and deliver the following concluding message:

Today we have considered the light of Advent. We've discovered that we need to remember to be still and wait. We need to prepare and pray. We need to give and shine.

Take some time now to talk with your group about ways that you celebrate during Advent. How can you all focus your attention Jesus?

Perhaps there are certain traditions or objects that might help you to spend time with God. For example (*hold up each item as you mention it*):
an advent wreath
daily advent prayers (*calendar*)
lighting a candle every day
or you might have some other ideas!

Let's celebrate together and give thanks to God for Jesus as we look forward to Christmas.

Invite several adults to come forward, take a party popper and, on the count of 3, release it. Invite the whole congregation to shout together: 'Thank you, God, for Jesus. Amen!'

FAMILY FUN DAYS

02

FAMILY FUN DAY
TANGRAM TIDINGS

A family event with tables of activities to explore. At each table participants will be invited to create something to help them understand more of the Christmas story. Each table will have someone present to facilitate and help with the activity. The event will end with a short interactive talk to summarise the theme.

YOU WILL NEED:
- a square sheet of card with tangram pattern from page 94 for each participant
- tables set up with helpers, and with materials listed in text

As each family arrives, give out a tangram sheet for each participant. Direct each family group to begin at Table 1.

TABLE 1

You will need: scissors, copy of patterns for tangram alphabet, printed out Bible verse, acrylic paints and felt-tip pens, mini acrylic canvases

Instructions:

1 Invite everyone to cut out their tangram pieces and then, using all the pieces, try to create the first letter of their name.

2 Explain that Jesus said: 'I am the Alpha and the Omega, the first and the last, the beginning and the end' (Revelation 22:13). Alpha and Omega are the first and last letters of the Greek alphabet, so that's like saying I am A to Z. Jesus was there at the beginning of the world and will be there at the end. He is like a circle with no end or beginning. He loves each one of us whatever letter our name begins with!

3 Encourage the participants to use mini acrylic canvas and acrylic paint or felt-tip pens to draw their own initial letter or a circle or heart, and decorate with painted patterns.

TABLE 2

You will need: wet wipes, paper plates, plastic bags, triangle shortbread pieces, after dinner mints, round sweets, eg flying saucers or marshmallows, tangram instructions for angel and Mary from page 94

Instructions:

1 Using all of the tangram pieces for each character, challenge everyone to try to create an angel and Mary (instructions are on page 94).

2 Retell the story of the angel's visit to Mary from Luke 1: 26–38.

3 Facilitate the creation of edible angels, using a triangle of shortbread for the body, after dinner mints cut into triangles for wings and a flying saucer or marshmallow for the head.

4 Make sure you take hygiene issues and any allergies into account for this activity.

TABLE 3

You will need: tangram instructions for stable and manger from pages 94 and 95, MDF wooden stars (available from most craft shops), decopatch papers and glue, small glue brushes, wet wipes

Instructions:

1 Using all of the tangram pieces for each, challenge everyone to try to create the stable and the manger (instructions are on pages 94 and 95).

2 Retell the story of Mary and Joseph travelling to Bethlehem, and Jesus being born in a stable.

3 Help the participants to decorate wooden stars with torn decopatch patterned paper. Tear the paper into small pieces. Put glue on the star. Pick up a piece of decopatch paper with the gluey brush, position on wooden star and repeat, overlapping all pieces until the star is covered. Ensure glue is over the top of the papers as well to seal.

TABLE 4

You will need: tangram instructions for shepherds and flying angel from page 95, decorative box or treasure chest, small blank cards, colouring pencils and felt-tip pens

Instructions:

1 Using all of the tangram pieces for each, challenge everyone to try to create the shepherds and flying angel (instructions are on page 95).

2 Retell the story of the shepherds from Luke 2:8–20.

3 Explain that the shepherds left their sheep to visit Jesus. They had nothing to take to Jesus except themselves. Invite the participants to consider the question: 'What would you bring to Jesus today?'

4 Invite the participants to draw a picture of whatever they would bring to Jesus on a small blank card, and perhaps write a prayer inside their card. Then invite everyone to place their cards in the treasure chest as a prayer offering.

TABLE 5

You will need: tangram instructions for magi and camel from page 95, coloured card approximately 30cm x 15cm with two holes punched at the top and bottom, metallic thread or ribbon, different coloured crowns cut from craft foam, stick on jewels, craft foam shapes and oddments

Instructions:

1 Using all of the tangram pieces for each, challenge everyone to try to create the magi and camel (instructions are on page 95).

2 Retell the story of the magi from Matthew 2:1–12.

3 Help the participants to create a card hanging with three crowns. Draw a crown on each of three pieces of card, and then place the cards on the table so that the crowns will fit one under another. Decorate the crowns with jewels and foam shapes. Join the crown cards together with pieces of metallic thread or ribbon. Add metallic thread for a hanging loop at the top.

END TALK

After a suitable time, gather the group together and recap what they have done, using the tangrams and craft activities:

1 Explain that the story does not end with the magi visiting Jesus. Ask if anyone can remember anything about Jesus' adult life.

2 Creating a candle from large tangram pieces, explain that Jesus came to earth to be like a light that would show people the way to God.

3 Creating a cross from the tangram pieces, explain that Jesus was born for a special purpose. God sent his Son, Jesus, to die on a cross and be raised to life again for us, so that we could be God's friend for ever.

4 Finish by giving out a sheet with the tangram shapes on so that families can tell the stories themselves.

MARBLED NATIVITY SCENE TEMPLATES

NAMES OF JESUS DECORATION

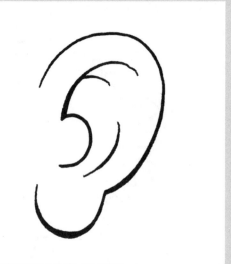

MAGI HEAD

MAGI CROWN

MAGI BODY

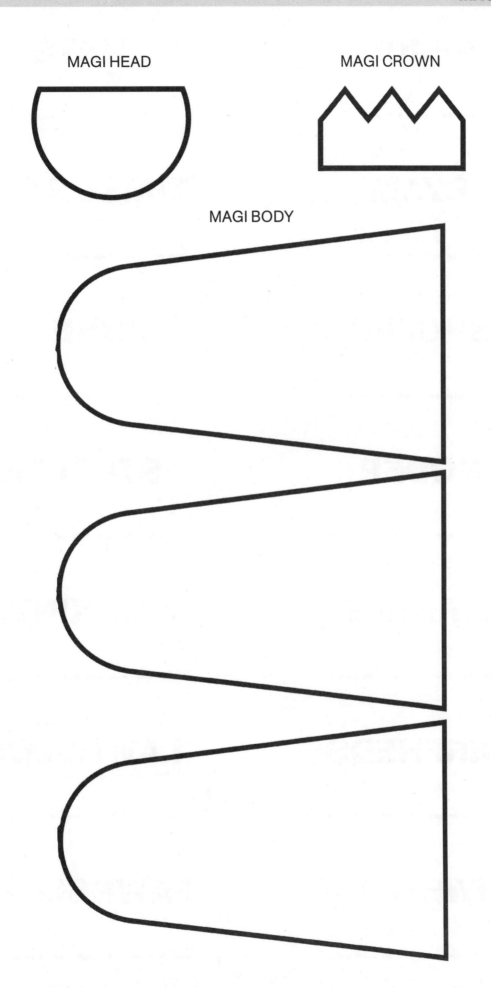

CHRISTMAS ANAGRAMS

SEJUS	**RATS**
_ _ _ _ _	_ _ _ _
RYAM	**TIMSCRASH**
_ _ _ _	_ _ _ _ _ _ _ _ _
SPOJEH	**UBBEAL**
_ _ _ _ _ _	_ _ _ _ _ _
HODER	**STREPEN**
_ _ _ _ _	_ _ _ _ _ _ _
BIRAGLE	**GOCKINTS**
_ _ _ _ _ _ _	_ _ _ _ _ _ _ _
HERPHEDS	**LAWNSLOB**
_ _ _ _ _ _ _ _	_ _ _ _ _ _ _ _
SIWE NMA	**FAWNSLOKE**
_ _ _ _ _ _ _	_ _ _ _ _ _ _ _ _

CHRISTMAS BOARD GAME

| START | 1 | 2 | Mary gets a visit from an angel! Go forward 2. | 4 | 5 | 6 | Mary finds out she will have a baby – God's Son! Go forward 2. |

| 8 |

| 15 | Joseph has an angel dream! Throw again. | 13 | 12 | 11 | Joseph decides to call off his wedding with Mary. Go back 2 | 9 |

| 16 |

| 17 | Mary and Joseph get married. | 19 | 20 | The Emperor organises a census. | 22 | 23 |

| 24 |

| 31 | In Bethlehem, there's no place to stay for Mary and Joseph. Miss a turn. | 29 | 28 | 27 | Joseph has to go to Bethlehem to be counted. | 25 |

| 32 |

| 33 | 34 | Finally, Jesus is born and laid in a manger. Go forward 2. | 36 | 37 | 38 | Some shepherds get a host of angel visitors! Miss a turn to watch! |

| 40 |

| 47 | 46 | Wise men travel to Jerusalem to find out more. | 44 | 43 | Wise men see a star telling of Jesus' birth. Throw again. | 41 |

| 48 |

| King Herod is angry about the news of a new king. Go back 3. | 50 | Wise men find Jesus, Mary and Joseph in Bethlehem. Go forward 2. | 52 | 53 | Wise men give their presents of gold, frankincense and myrrh. Throw again. | 55 | END (OR IS IT?) |

 HAVE ANOTHER GO   MISS A GO   CHOOSE SOMEONE ELSE TO MISS A GO

C Carols, Crackers, Cake, Crib, Christ child

H Holly

R Reindeer

I Ivy, Immanuel

S Santa, Sleigh, Snowmen, Shopping

T Tinsel, Tree, Turkey

M Mince pies, Magi, Mistletoe

A Angels

S Stars, Shepherds, Stable, Sheep

T'was the night before Christmas

T'was the night before Christmas
and all through the town,
the little Lord Jesus?
He could not be found.

Everyone was so busy
with Christmas-time chores –
baking, decorating
and shopping in stores!

Not 'Away in a manger,
no crib for a bed',
but songs about Santa
dressed up in bright red.

Right up on the roof-top was
such a great clatter
as Dad hung the lights up,
perched on a ladder.

He hung lights that would flash and
bright lights that would twirl,
but what about Jesus,
the light of the world?

People's lives were so busy
with Christmas-time things…
No time to remember
Christ Jesus, the King.

The reason for the season?
It's Jesus' birthday
Put Christ back in Christmas
and have a great day!

Source unknown

AWE AND WONDER STAR

Angel

Mary

Inn and stable

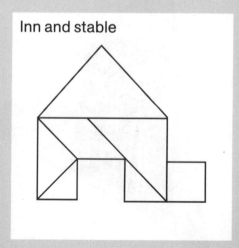

Angel flying

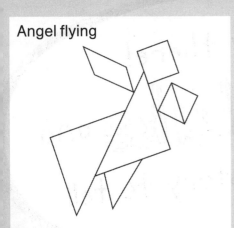

Camel

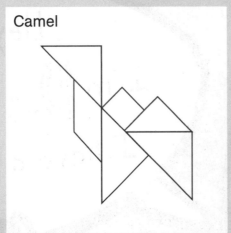

Candle

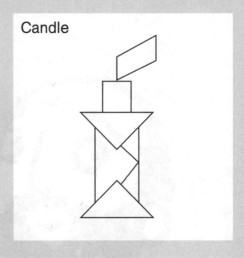

Cross

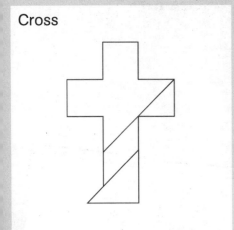

Kneeling magi

Kneeling shepherd

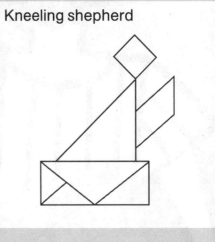

Magi 1

Magi 2

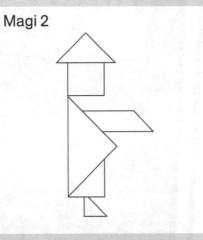

Manger

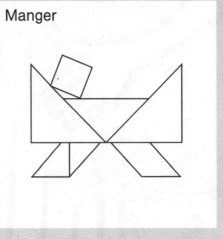

Running shepherd

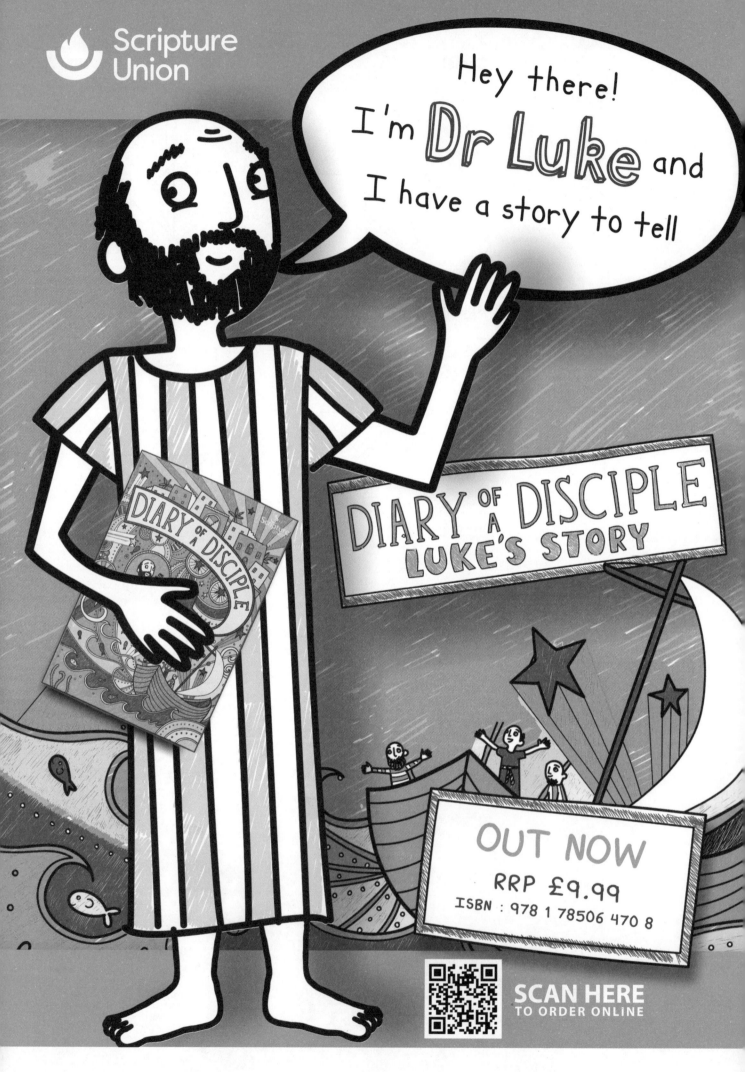